# SCOTT, FORESMAN
# TREASURES
## OF THE
# WORLD

## Literature and Source Readings for World History

# SCOTT, FORESMAN
# TREASURES
# OF THE
# WORLD

## Literature and Source Readings for World History

**Donna Maier** • **Heidi Roupp**

### Scott, Foresman and Company

Editorial Offices: Glenview, Illinois
Regional Offices: Sunnyvale, California • Atlanta, Georgia
Glenview, Illinois • Oakland, New Jersey • Dallas, Texas

*Facing title page:* Between 1508 and 1512, Michelangelo was employed in decorating the ceiling of the Sistine Chapel in Rome with frescoes (paintings done on fresh plaster). Among the most famous figures of the Sistine ceiling is the Libyan Sibyl, shown in this detail. The sibyls [sib′əlz] were ten prophetesses in Classical mythology who were associated with different places in the ancient world.

**Donna Maier** is a professor of history at the University of Northern Iowa. She has served as an African studies consultant for encyclopedia and trade book publishers. She has traveled and studied widely in Africa, the Middle East, and Europe. The author of a number of books and articles on African culture, she is presently lecturing in African history and world history.

**Heidi Roupp** is a history teacher at Aspen High School, Aspen, Colorado. Currently Regional Director of the Colorado Council for Social Studies and a member of the National Executive Council of the World History Association, she has participated in many panels on the teaching of world history. She has traveled widely and done postgraduate work in East Asian Studies.

The authors and editors of *Treasures of the World* would like to acknowledge the contributions of the following young people, students at Aspen High School, Aspen, Colorado, who read, discussed, and evaluated materials proposed for inclusion in the book, as well as suggesting questions and activities that they felt would interest students.

Chris Anderson
Trevi M. Burkholder
Chamisa J. Lopez Lamm
Mike MacKenzie
Erik Rudolph
Jennifer Spaulding
Bethany Wilkes

# Table of Contents

A San rock painting shows elands pursued by a hunter.

A prince hunting with hounds is shown in a 16th-century Persian manuscript.

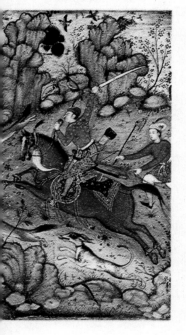

The arms of Pope Clement VII appear on the goldwork by Cellini at the top. Above is a detail of an Aztec featherwork shield.

A portrait of British statesman Joseph Chamberlain appears at the top. A detail of a cartoon by George Cruikshank of the Peterloo Massacre is shown above.

A modern Saudi oil engineer at work appears above. Irish civil-rights activist Bernadette Devlin is shown below with Ulster children.

# To the Student

What are our basic human rights? What are the limits to the use of capital punishment? Should nuclear weapons ever be used? Your answers to questions such as these will shape the 21st century. The way things are today is the result of many people's answers to these questions and others like them. You deserve to know who those people were, to understand how and why they arrived at their answers, and to judge the decisions they made which determined the present.

History is more than just lecture and memorization. At its best, history requires all of your brain cells, plus a few of your neighbor's. When you and others analyze, defend, question, listen, and think about how things are and how they should be, what results is a kind of "athletic history."

One way to practice this kind of history is to exercise a whole group of brains at one time in a team effort of intellectual volleyball. One person serves a question over the net that gets received by someone with an idea. That person sets to someone else, who elaborates on or challenges the idea, and who changes the direction of play. It's the volley—the back and forth activity—that makes the game. The best discussions involve all of the players, not just a few superstars. Positions rotate so that everyone gets a chance. New questions get served to a variety of players, and new points are made.

A few words of caution—for athletic history to work, the members of the team need to trust one another. Personal attacks are out-of-bounds because they destroy morale and discourage discussion. A class discussion is a group effort to find new ideas and test their validity. Careful listening and respect for your teammates are the keys to winning new insights.

Do come to class prepared. Read each selection carefully. Although the questions at the end of each selection are intended for discussion, not for writing, you may want to jot down notes or rough out your own questions. Aim for a discussion that flows like one outside of class—one that doesn't need hand-raising or a teacher serving as referee. At the end of class spend a few minutes as a group summarizing the ideas, the quotations, the evidence worth remembering. Evaluate your discussion. In other words, review the game films.

If you work hard as a team, you will have winning ideas that will remain with you. Good luck!

Heidi Roupp

## A Note on the Editing of the Readings

Words in brackets([ ]) indicate changes in the original wording or an explanation added for clarity. Ellipses ( . . . ) indicate omissions from the original text. Spelling and punctuation have been modernized. Pronunciations are from the *Scott, Foresman Advanced Dictionary*. The pronunciation symbols used are shown in the Pronunciation Key below.

| a hat | i it | oi oil | ch child | a in about |
|---|---|---|---|---|
| ā age | ī ice | ou out | ng long | e in taken |
| ä far | o hot | u cup | sh she | i in pencil |
| e let | ō open | ù put | th thin | o in lemon |
| ē equal | ô order | ü rule | ᵺ then | u in circus |
| ėr term | | | zh measure | < = derived from |

1

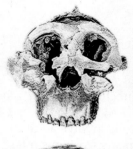

Above left is the "Zinj" skull after careful piecing together. The lower jaw was never found. Below left is "Zinj" as he may have looked in life. At the right is Mary Leakey starting to uncover the "Zinj" skull in 1959, accompanied by her Dalmations, Sally and Victoria.

# Mary Leakey Finds Zinjanthropus

**TIME FRAME**
*Mid-20th century*
**GEOGRAPHIC SETTING**
*East Africa*

Mary and Louis Leakey were two archaeologists who married and devoted their professional lives to searching for prehistoric remains in East Africa. Prehistoric archaeologists are scientists who study the remains of early humans, such as fossils and tools, in the field as well as in the laboratories of museums. Unlike many students of prehistory earlier in this century, the Leakeys believed that human beings came originally from Africa. They concentrated their search for evidence of early humans in East Africa, especially in a valley in what is now Tanzania [tan′zə nē′ə] called Olduvai [ol′dü vā′] Gorge. The most significant find they made was a hominid [hom′ə nid] skull that has been variously dated at between 1.75 and 2 million years old. The Leakeys called the fossil species *Zinjanthropus* [zin jan′thrə pəs; from Arabic *Zinj* meaning "East Africa" and Greek *anthrōpos* meaning "human being"]. (Today this fossil species is referred to as *Australopithecus boisei*.) Although older examples of hominids have been found, "Zinj," as the Leakeys nicknamed their find, was important because it was found *in situ* [in sī′tü; from Latin meaning "in its original place"]. Applied to *Zinjanthropus*, this phrase means that the fossil was found among the remains of animals and evidence of tool-making that demonstrated how these early hominids lived. The following is an excerpt from Mary Leakey's account of how she discovered *Zinjanthropus*.

W e returned to Olduvai [in 1959] for only a short stay, determined to turn our attention to the oldest levels there, those belonging to Bed 1. But
5 where, among all the many miles, should we make a start?

. . . Then Louis got an attack of 'flu and retired to bed, and so it came about that on the morning of 17 July I went
10 out by myself, with the two Dalmatians, Sally and Victoria, to see what I could find of interest at nearby Bed 1 exposures. I turned my steps towards a site not far west of the junction of the two
15 gorges, where we knew that bones and stone artifacts were fairly common on the surface of Bed 1 sediments. . . .

There was indeed plenty of material lying on the eroded surface [there], 20 some no doubt as a result of the rains earlier that year. But one scrap of bone that caught and held my eye was not lying loose on the surface but projecting from beneath. It seemed to be part of a 25 skull, including a mastoid process (the bony projection below the ear). It had a hominid look, but the bones seemed enormously thick—too thick, surely. I carefully brushed away a little of the 30 deposit, and then I could see parts of two large teeth in place in the upper jaw. They *were* hominid. It was a hominid skull, apparently *in situ,* and there was a lot of it there. I rushed back to camp to 35 tell Louis, who leaped out of bed, and then we were soon back at the site, looking at my find together. . . . Zinjanthropus had come into our lives. . . .

We devoted the rest of our time at 40 Olduvai in 1959 to extracting it, recovering every fragment we could find by sieving and washing the soil, and to demonstrating that it was indeed *in situ* on what was clearly part of an 45 extensive living floor with many stone artifacts and animal bones. . . . I . . . devoted myself to the task of fitting the fragments of the skull back together.

## Discussing the Reading

1. How "lucky" was Mary Leakey? How did her background as a prehistoric archaeologist and her belief in the African origins of early humans prepare her to make her discovery?

2. If the rains had washed Zinj out of the soil and carried the fossil to another spot where a tourist found it and presented it to a museum, would this have been a discovery as great as Mary Leakey's?

**CRITICAL THINKING**
**Evaluating Sources of Information**

Does this reading more properly belong in a science text than a history text? Why or why not?

# Rock Art of the San

# 1B

**TIME FRAME**
*Mid-20th century*

**GEOGRAPHIC SETTING**
*Southern Africa*

Prehistoric rock art has been found all over the world. As these paintings and engravings were the creation of hunting and gathering societies, animals and hunters are their most common themes, and the graceful, stylized treatments of these themes in examples of rock art from throughout the world are startling in their similarity. Therefore, it is likely that when in 1930, the wife of a British colonial official in southern Africa persuaded Mapote [mä pō′tā], an elderly individual of the San (or Bushman) people, one of the last hunting and gathering groups, to do some rock paintings for her, his methods were not very different from those of prehistoric peoples.

When Mapote arrived at [the Residency] I asked him if he would do some painting for me. He said that it was a very long time since he had 5 painted and he had thought of asking some old friend to join him. "I will ask . . . ," he said. "I will ask. . . ." He put his hand over his eyes and said again, "I will ask. . . ." Then he took his 10 hand from his eyes, looked at me and said, "They are all dead that I could ask." But as he set to work it all came back to him, like riding a bicycle again after many years.

In a part of the Residency grounds there were several blocks of stone of different sizes which had been left there after the building of the house. He ran his fingers over a number of them and seemed as fussy about choosing the one he liked as an artist is in selecting his paper or canvas. The stone had to be fairly porous so as to absorb the pigment and smooth enough on which to work. The best stone on which to paint is [the] smooth sandstone used for sharpening knives.

I asked him to paint two pictures . . . and he ultimately selected two stones and brought them onto the verandah. Then he disappeared for some time, eventually returning with his paint brushes, consisting of bird feathers stuck into the ends of tiny reeds.

Mapote could not remember what substance was employed as the white pigment but he thought it was [a sticky clay] which is used by . . . girls to smear their bodies at initiation. Mapote mixed it with the thick white juice from the stem of a plant. The most prevalent colors in the rock paintings are reddish-brown, black, and white. The brown was probably . . . a black earth used for adorning earthenware pots. Possibly mixing it with blood or other substance it might become brown. For the black pigment Mapote burnt some sticks and used the charcoal mixed with water. After collecting his various materials together he then announced that he required the blood of a freshly killed eland [ē'lənd; a large African antelope]. Not having an eland for him, early next morning I sent to the local butcher for a cup of freshly killed ox blood. The blood must be fresh, otherwise it will coagulate and will not mix with the pigment or soak into the rock. This indicates that the Bushman paintings must have been executed immediately after a successful hunt and a good meal, thus

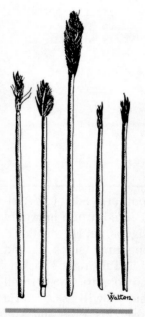

Using the brushes pictured above, Mapote produced paintings like the San rock art on the right, which shows elands pursued by a hunter.

prompting cheerful and energetic thoughts. It also provides an added
65 reason why the older paintings are better than those of later days when the Bushmen were often harassed and hungry.

[Mapote] said he would paint an
70 eland, as the Bushmen of that part of the country were of the eland. . . . It was most interesting watching him use his little feather brush. He began . . . in a rather peculiar way, starting from the
75 animal's chest and moving his brush along smoothly without the slightest hesitation. He used a different brush for each color.

Next day I asked Mapote to do some
80 paintings on the big rock which rises abruptly in the Residency grounds. . . . But much water pours down that rock in the rainy season. He did not like the idea of putting his paintings there because
85 he said that, although the colors were completely sun-proof for ages, they were not entirely rain-proof. The Bushmen preferred putting their paintings inside the caves or rock-shelters
90 and he wanted to put his paintings in a

little cave which was just above the doctor's garden. . . . I was not sure what the reactions of the doctor might be to Bushman paintings so Mapote put them
95 on the exposed [rock] and, as he feared, . . . they have now almost completely weathered away.

## Discussing the Reading

1. Mapote was unable to think of a living member of his people to whom he could turn for help in producing the paintings the Englishwoman requested of him. What does this suggest about the traditions of the society from which he came?

2. What inferences did the Englishwoman draw from the fact that pigments used in San paintings were mixed with fresh blood? (Look at lines 59–68.)

**CRITICAL THINKING**
**Recognizing Values**

Would you classify a rock painting as imaginative art, historical record, or religious expression? Explain your answer.

# Schooldays in Sumer

**TIME FRAME**
*2000 B.C.*

**GEOGRAPHIC SETTING**
*Mesopotamia*

By about 2500 B.C. most Sumerian cities had a "tablet house," or writing school, where clever boys—the future administrators of the city-state—learned to inscribe cuneiform [kyü nē′ə fôrm] script with a wedge-shaped reed stylus on clay tablets. The "composition" below, which is an account of a day spent by a Sumerian schoolboy, comes from a cuneiform tablet that dates from around 2000 B.C.

T he composition, which was no doubt the creation of one of the

"professors" in the "tablet house," begins with a direct question to the
5 pupil: "Schoolboy, where did you go from earliest days?" The boy answers: "I went to school." The author then asks: "What did you do in school?" There follows the pupil's reply . . . : "I
10 recited my tablet, ate my lunch, prepared my [new] tablet, wrote it, finished it; then they assigned me my oral work, and in the afternoon they assigned me my written work. When school was dis-
15 missed, I went home, entered the

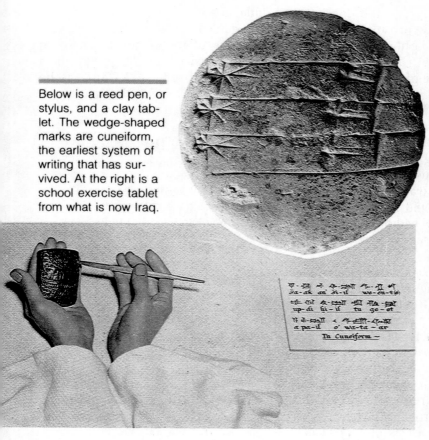

Below is a reed pen, or stylus, and a clay tablet. The wedge-shaped marks are cuneiform, the earliest system of writing that has survived. At the right is a school exercise tablet from what is now Iraq.

In Cuneiform –

of the gate. Worst of all, the teacher said to him, "Your hand [copy] is not satisfactory," and caned him. This seems to have been too much for the lad, and he suggests to his father that it might be a good idea to invite the teacher home. . . . "To that which the schoolboy said, his father gave heed. The teacher was brought from school, and after entering the house he was seated in the seat of honor. The schoolboy attended and served him, and whatever he had learned of the art of tablet-writing he unfolded to his father."

The father then wined and dined the teacher, "dressed him in a new garment, gave him a gift, put a ring on his hand." Warmed by this generosity, the teacher reassures the aspiring scribe in poetic words, which read in part: "Young man, because you did not neglect my word, did not forsake it, may you reach the pinnacle of the scribal art, may you achieve it completely."

house, and found my father sitting there. I told my father of my written work, then recited my tablet to him, and my father was delighted. . . . When I awoke early in the morning, I faced my mother and said to her: 'Give me my lunch, I want to go to school.' My mother gave me two 'rolls' and I set out; my mother gave me two 'rolls' and I went to school. In school the monitor in charge said to me, 'Why are you late?' Afraid and with pounding heart, I entered before my teacher and made a respectful curtsy."

But curtsy or not, it seems to have been a bad day for this pupil. He had to take canings from the various members of the school staff for such indiscretions as talking, standing up, and walking out

## Discussing the Reading

1. Was the "wining and dining" of the teacher a bribe or a legitimate way of dealing with the student's problems?

2. Is corporal punishment an effective way to motivate a student? Why or why not?

**CRITICAL THINKING**
**Analyzing Comparisons**

Compare the character of education in Sumer with that which it has in modern America. In analyzing the similarities and differences, consider the following questions: Who does each society try to educate—an elite or everyone? What is the role of the teacher in each society? What are the benefits of education in each society, both for the individual and for the society as a whole?

# An Egyptian Vision of Judgment

**TIME FRAME**
*1500* B.C.

**GEOGRAPHIC SETTING**
*Egypt*

Below is a portion of the *Book of the Dead*. In the upper left corner is the deceased, kneeling before a row of gods. Below the deceased is shown being judged at the scale of Maat, the goddess of truth. The deceased is then escorted to meet Osiris, god of the dead, seated on the throne at the right.

From the beginning of their civilization, the Egyptians believed in a life after death. At first this afterlife was thought to be available only to kings. Over the centuries, however, the Egyptians came to believe that if a person led a moral life and the correct rituals were performed, anyone could attain immortality. The Egyptian vision of judgment pictured the god Osiris [ō sī′ris], ruler of the world of the dead, sitting in the Hall of Maat [ma ät′], or "truth." The judge of the dead, Osiris met an individual's soul as it crossed over from the earthly world and decided whether it deserved immortality. Many handbooks were written to advise people what they needed to say to Osiris at this final judgment. One of the most famous was written about 1500 B.C. and is known as the *Book of the Dead*. In the following excerpt from the *Book of the Dead*, a person's soul faces Osiris and lists all the sins this individual had avoided during life. The "Hall of the Two Truths" referred to here is the Hall of Maat. The majority of the "forty-two gods" mentioned are minor deities.

H ail to you, great God, Lord of the Two Truths!
I have come to you, my Lord,
I was brought to see your beauty.
5 I know you, I know the names of the forty-two gods,
Who are with you in the Hall of the Two Truths,
Who live by warding off evildoers,
10 Who drink of their blood,
On that day of judging characters before [Osiris]. . . .
I have not done crimes against people,
15 I have not mistreated cattle, . . .
I have not blasphemed a god,
I have not robbed the poor.
I have not done what the god abhors,
20 I have not maligned a servant to his master.
I have not caused pain,
I have not caused tears.

I have not killed,
25 I have not ordered to kill,
I have not made anyone suffer.
I have not damaged the offerings in
the temples, . . .
I have not added to the weight of the
30 balance,
I have not falsified the plummet of
the scales.
I have not taken milk from the mouth
of children,
35 I have not deprived cattle of their
pasture.

I have not snared birds in the reeds
of the gods,
I have not caught fish in their ponds.
40 I have not held back water in its
seasons,
I have not dammed a flowing
stream, . . .
I am pure, I am pure, I am pure, I am
45 pure! . . .
No evil shall befall me in this land,
In this Hall of the Two Truths;
For I know the names of the gods in it,
The followers of the great God!

## Discussing the Reading

1. Lines 13–43 detail what ancient Egyptians saw as sins. Determine general categories of sins and divide those listed in the *Book of the Dead* into these categories.

2. Given what they saw as sins, what kind of concerns did the ancient Egyptians have about their daily lives?

**CRITICAL THINKING**
**Making Generalizations**

Based on this excerpt from the *Book of the Dead*, what kind of a society was ancient Egypt? How did that society differ in values from ours? Which of the acts considered sinful by the ancient Egyptians would still be unacceptable behavior today?

# The Israelites Get a King

3A

**TIME FRAME**
*Late 11th century* B.C.

**GEOGRAPHIC SETTING**
*Canaan*

When the Israelites returned from Egypt to Canaan [kā′nən], the region between the Jordan River and the Mediterranean Sea, they began a long struggle with a number of Canaanite peoples. At this period the Israelites had no permanent rulers, but were governed by local temporary military leaders called judges. As the Old Testament observes, "In those days there was no king in Israel; every man did what was right in his own eye." Growing dissatisfied with this situation, the Israelites went to their current leader, Samuel, and asked him to give them a king like the Canaanite peoples had. He agreed, but in the following passage from the Old Testament he warned them of the dangers of a king.

When Samuel became old, he made his sons judges over Israel. . . . Yet his sons did not walk in his ways, but turned aside after gain; they
5 took bribes and perverted justice.

Then all the elders of Israel gathered together and came to Samuel at Ramah, and said to him, "Behold, you are old and your sons do not walk in your ways;
10 now appoint for us a king to govern us like all the nations." But the thing displeased Samuel when they said, "Give us a king to govern us." . . .

He said, "These will be the ways of
15 the king who will reign over you: he will

Standing before the prophet and judge Samuel, the men of Israel, pictured in this illustration from a 13th-century French manuscript, request that he give them a king.

take your sons and appoint them to his chariots and to be his horsemen, and to run before his chariots; and he will appoint for himself commanders of
20 thousands and commanders of fifties, and some to plow his ground and to reap his harvest, and to make his implements of war and the equipment of his chariots. He will take your daughters to
25 be perfumers and cooks and bakers. He will take the best of your fields and vineyards and olive orchards and give them to his servants. He will take the tenth of your grain and of your vineyards and
30 give it to his officers and to his servants. He will take your menservants and maidservants, and the best of your cattle and your asses, and put them to his work. He will take the tenth of your
35 flocks, and you shall be his slaves. And in that day you will cry out because of your king, whom you have chosen for yourselves; but the Lord will not answer you in that day."
40 But the people refused to listen to the voice of Samuel; and they said, "No! but we will have a king over us, that we also may be like all the nations, and that our king may govern us and go out before us
45 and fight our battles." And when Samuel had heard all the words of the people, he repeated them in the ears of the Lord. And the Lord said to Samuel, "Hearken to their voice, and make them
50 a king."

## Discussing the Reading

1. What prompted the Israelites to ask Samuel to give them a king?
2. What were Samuel's objections to a king for Israel?

### CRITICAL THINKING
### Analyzing Comparisons

Compare the advantages of a strong central government to those of a weak one. Use your answer to questions 1 and 2 above in analyzing the two types of government.

# The Assyrians Destroy Ancient Babylon

3B

**TIME FRAME**
*Early 7th century* B.C.

**GEOGRAPHIC SETTING**
*Mesopotamia*

The Assyrians conquered most of their empire in the Fertile Crescent in the 8th century B.C. They relied on their brutal army to control the peoples they conquered. Their own records boast of torture, enslavement, and mass deportation of their defeated enemies. One of their favorite tactics was to place the heads of their many victims on stakes outside a city's wall to remind the surviving citizens what would happen if they rebelled. This did not prevent people from trying to throw off the Assyrian yoke, and the most famous revolt was that of the great and ancient city of Babylon in 689 B.C. The Assyrian king Sennacherib [sə nak'ər ib] took his revenge by not only killing the people of Babylon, but destroying the city itself, as he told us in his own words.

I completely invested that city, with mines and [siegecraft] my hands [took the city]. . . . With their corpses I filled the city squares. Shuzubu, king of
5 Babylonia, together with his family and his [nobles], I carried off alive into my land. The wealth of that city—silver, gold, precious stones, property and goods, I doled out to my people and
10 they made it their own. The gods dwelling therein—the hands of my

people took them, and then smashed them. Their property and goods they seized. . . .

15 The city and its houses, from its foundation to its top, I destroyed, I devastated, I burned with fire. The wall and outer wall, temples and gods, temple towers of brick and earth, as many as 20 there were, I razed and dumped them into the Arahtu Canal. Through the midst of that city I dug canals, I flooded its site with water, and the very foundations thereof I destroyed. I made its 25 destruction more complete than that by a flood. That in days to come the site of that city, and its temples and gods, might not be remembered, I completely blotted it out with floods of water and 30 made it like a meadow. . . .

After I had destroyed Babylon, had smashed the gods thereof, and had struck down its people with the sword—that the ground of that city 35 might be carried off, I removed its ground and had it carried to the Euphrates and on to the sea.

At the left below is a map of the ancient Mesopotamian city of Nippur from a clay tablet. On the right is a drawing by the 19th-century British archaeologist Austen Henry Layard of a decoration in carved stone from the Assyrian capital of Nineveh. The carving shows a scene within a captured fortress. In the upper part a king is pictured on his throne. In the lower part are cutaway views of tents showing soldiers engaged in everyday tasks.

## Discussing the Reading

1. What was Sennacherib's policy for ruling Babylon?
2. How did he implement his policy? What were the advantages and disadvantages of such a policy?

**CRITICAL THINKING**
**Predicting Effects**

Do you think Sennacherib's policy was effective in ending revolt? Why or why not? What other strategies could he have used?

# Lycurgus Reforms Sparta

**TIME FRAME**
*9th century* B.C.

**GEOGRAPHIC SETTING**
*Greece*

Spartans claimed that sometime in the 9th century B.C. a great leader called Lycurgus [lī kér′gəs] decreed a number of rules and laws that set the pattern for the constitution of Sparta down to the 4th century. Scholars today feel that no one person could have accomplished all with which Lycurgus is credited. The Greek historian Plutarch [plü′tärk] (A.D. 46?–120?) agreed, but after examining all the ancient sources concluded that even if the Lycurgan reforms were the accomplishment of several leaders, the accomplishment was no less remarkable.

The ... boldest of Lycurgus's reforms was the redistribution of the land. Great inequalities existed, many poor and needy people had become a
5 burden to the state, while wealth had got into a very few hands. Lycurgus abolished all the mass of pride, envy, crime, and luxury, which flowed from those old and more terrible evils of
10 riches and poverty, by inducing all landowners to offer their estates for redistribution, and prevailing upon them to live on equal terms one with another, and with equal incomes. . . .
15 He desired to distribute movable property also, in order completely to do away with inequality; but, seeing that actually to take away these things would be a most unpopular measure, he
20 managed by a different method to put an end to all ostentation in these matters. First of all, he abolished the use of gold and silver money, and made iron money alone legal; and this he made of
25 great size and weight, and small value, so that the equivalent for ten minae [mī′nē] required a great room for its stowage, and a yoke of oxen to draw it. As soon as this was established, many
30 sorts of crime became unknown in [Sparta]. For who would steal, or take as a bribe or deny that he possessed, or take by force a mass of iron which he could not conceal, which no one envied
35 him for possessing, which he could not even break up and so make use of. . . .

Wrapped in his cloak, and with his hair in long braids emerging from beneath his crested helmet, a Spartan warrior is depicted in this Greek bronze statue, which dates from the 6th century B.C.

A Spartan gravestone from the 6th century B.C. shows a dead couple, with two tiny figures, probably representing their descendants, bringing offerings to them.

[As a second reform, Lycurgus expelled all workers employed in the creation of luxury goods.] Wishing still further to put down luxury and take away the desire for riches, he introduced the third and the most admirable of his reforms, that of the common dining table. At this the people were to meet and dine together upon a fixed allowance of food, and not to live in their own homes, lolling on expensive couches at rich tables. . . .

Considering education to be the most important and the noblest work of a lawgiver, he began at the very beginning, and regulated marriages and the birth of children. . . . He strengthened the bodies of the girls by exercise in running, wrestling, and hurling [the discus] or javelins, in order that their children might spring from a healthy source and so grow up strong, and that they themselves might have strength, so as easily to endure the pains of childbirth. He did away with all affectation of seclusion and retirement among the women, and ordained that the girls, no less than the boys, . . . value good health, and . . . love honor and courage no less than the men. This it was that made them speak and think as we are told [that] Gorgo, the wife of Leonidas, did. Some foreign lady, it seems, said to her, "You [Spartan] women are the only ones that rule men." She answered, "Yes, for we alone give birth to men." . . .

A father had not the right of bringing up his offspring but had to carry it to a certain place called Lesche [les'kē], where the elders of the tribe sat in judgment upon the child. If they thought it well-built and strong, they ordered the father to bring it up . . . but if it was mean-looking or misshapen, they sent it away to the place called the Exposure [where it died]. . . .

Nor was each man allowed to bring
85 up and educate his son as he chose, but as soon as they were seven years of age [Lycurgus] received them from their parents, and enrolled them in companies. Here they lived and [ate] in
90 common, and were associated for play and for work. . . . They learned their letters, because they are necessary, but all the rest of their education was meant to teach them to obey with cheerfulness,
95 to endure labors, and to win battles. As they grew older their training became more severe; [their heads] were closely shorn and [they were] taught to walk barefooted and to play naked. They
100 wore no tunic after their twelfth year, but received one garment for all the year round. . . .

The training of the Spartan youth continued till their manhood. No one 105 was permitted to live according to his own pleasure, but they lived in the city as if in a camp, with a fixed diet and fixed public duties, thinking themselves to belong not to themselves but to their 110 country.

## Discussing the Reading

1. What reforms did Lycurgus institute in Sparta?

2. What were the difficulties in instituting reforms?

3. Compare the position of women in ancient Sparta to their position in the contemporary United States.

### CRITICAL THINKING
### Assessing Cause and Effect

How did the Spartan educational system help achieve the goals of the Lycurgan reforms?

# Alexander's Vision of Empire

4B

**TIME FRAME**
*Mid-4th century* B.C.

**GEOGRAPHIC SETTING**
*From Greece to India*

By 323 B.C., when he was thirty-three years old, Alexander the Great had conquered a vast empire. Although he was clearly a skillful and gallant soldier, his ability to administer his empire was never tested because of his early death. Nevertheless, during the last few years of his life Alexander took many actions which lead some scholars to believe that he had a vision of one world united under one law where all peoples would be treated equally regardless of race or culture. Alexander's biographer Plutarch had expressed this opinion already in the first century A.D. The *Republic* of the philosopher Zeno [zē′nō] (336?–264? B.C.), mentioned by Plutarch, is a work that deals with the nature of ideal government. Like all of Zeno's writings, it is now lost.

Moreover, the much-admired *Republic* of Zeno, the founder of the Stoic sect, may be summed up in this one main principle: that all the in-
5 habitants of this world of ours should not live differentiated by their respective rules of justice into separate cities and communities, but that we should consider all men to be of one commu-
10 nity and one [government], and that we should have a common life and an order common to us all, even as a herd that feeds together and shares the pasturage of a common field. This Zeno wrote,
15 giving shape to a dream or, as it were, shadowy picture of a well-ordered and

philosophic commonwealth; but it was Alexander who gave effect to the idea. For Alexander did not follow Aristotle's advice to treat the Greeks as if he were their leader, and other peoples as if he were their master; to have regard for the Greeks as for friends and kindred, but to conduct himself toward other peoples as though they were plants or animals; for to do so would have been to [burden] his leadership with numerous battles and banishments and [constant revolts]. But, as he believed that he came as a heaven-sent governor to all, and as a mediator for the whole world, those whom he could not persuade to unite with him, he conquered by force of arms, and he brought together into one body all men everywhere, uniting and mixing in one great loving cup, as it were, men's lives, their characters, their marriages, their very habits of life. He bade them all consider as their fatherland the whole inhabited earth, as their stronghold and protection his camp, as akin to them all good men, and as foreigners only the wicked; they should not distinguish between Grecian and foreigner by Grecian cloak and [shield], or [sword] and jacket; but the distinguishing mark of the Grecian should be seen in virtue, and that of the foreigner in iniquity; clothing and food, marriage and manner of life they should regard as common to all, being blended into one by ties of blood and children.

. . . For he did not overrun Asia like a robber nor was he minded to tear and rend it, as if it were booty and plunder bestowed by unexpected good fortune, after the manner in which Hannibal later descended upon Italy. . . . But Alexander desired to render all upon earth subject to one law of reason and one form of government and to reveal all men as one people, and to this purpose he made himself conform. But if the deity that sent down Alexander's soul into this world of ours had not recalled him quickly, one law would govern all mankind, and they all would look toward one rule of justice as though toward a common source of light. But as it is, that part of the world which has not looked upon Alexander has remained without sunlight.

Therefore, in the first place, the very plan and design of Alexander's expedition commends the man as a philosopher in his purpose not to win for himself luxury and extravagant living, but to win for all men concord and peace and community of interests.

Shown with ram's horns, identifying him with Zeus Ammon, a Greco-Egyptian god whose shrine was in the Libyan desert, the head of Alexander appears on this coin minted by Lysimachus (360?–281 B.C.), one of Alexander's generals and later king of Thrace, a country northeast of Greece.

**Discussing the Reading**

1. Who was more effective as a leader, Sennacherib (see Reading 3B) or Alexander? Explain your answer.

2. What risks did Alexander take as a leader in trying to establish a common world order?

3. Zeno compared human beings to "a herd that feeds together and shares the pasturage of a common field." In today's world, what issues relating to the "common field" require international cooperation to solve?

**CRITICAL THINKING**
**Predicting Effects**

If Alexander had lived longer, would he have succeeded in establishing a world government? Why or why not?

# A Satiric Portrait of Socrates

5A

**TIME FRAME**
*Late 5th century* B.C.

**GEOGRAPHIC SETTING**
*Greece*

The Greek playwright Aristophanes [ar'ə stof'ə nēz] wrote comedies in Athens in the 5th century B.C. Nothing and no one escaped his biting humor, including his contemporary, the philosopher Socrates [sok'rə tēz], whose practice of questioning established values made him unpopular. Aristophanes himself felt that traditional religion and morality were being undermined by thinkers like Socrates. In Aristophanes' play *The Clouds*, a farmer named Strepsiades [strep sē'ə dēz] is close to ruin because of his son's gambling debts at the horse races. Strepsiades tries to get his son Pheidippides [fī dip'ə dēz'; "lover of horses"] to enroll in Socrates' school, called the Thinkery, where he might learn a way out of debt.

---

**S**trepsiades: My boy, that little hovel is the Thinkery. Intellectuals live there.... What's more—for a fee, of course—they offer a course called "The
5 Technique of Winning Lawsuits." Honest or dishonest, it's all one.... My dearest boy, I implore you. Please go and study at the Thinkery.

**Pheidippides:** Study what?

10 **Strepsiades:** I've heard that they teach two kinds of Logic. One of them is called Philosophical, or Moral, Logic—whatever *that* may be. The other one is called Sophistic, or Socratic, Logic.
15 Now, if you could learn this second Logic, I wouldn't have to pay a penny of all those debts you've saddled me with.

**Pheidippides:** Count me out. I'd rather die. Why those vampires would
20 suck me dry. They'd scrape the tan right off my face. How could I face the fellows down at the track?... [Exit Pheidippides]

**Strepsiades:** I'm down, but not for
25 long. First I'll say a little prayer to the gods, and then I'll go and enroll at the Thinkery myself.... Throw open the Thinkery! Unbolt the door and let me see this wizard Socrates in person. Open
30 up! I'm MAD for education! ... [Strepsiades now enters the Thinkery and is shown about by a student who explains the various charts, maps, and instruments.... Strepsiades ... catches sight
35 of Socrates hanging in a basket overhead.] Who's that dangling up there in the basket?

**Student:** Himself.

**Strepsiades:** Who's Himself?

40 **Student:** Socrates.

**Strepsiades:** Socrates! ... O Socrates!

Above left are two terra-cotta statuettes of actors. On the right is a mosaic dating from the 3rd century B.C. that shows tragic and comic masks.

[No answer from the basket.] Yoohoo, Socrates!

Socrates [from a great height]: Well, creature of a day?

Strepsiades: What in the world are you doing up there?

Socrates: Ah, sir, I walk upon the air and look down upon the sun from a superior standpoint.

Strepsiades: Well, I suppose it's better that you sneer at the gods from a basket up in the air than do it down here on the ground. . . . O dear little Socrates, please come down. Lower away, and teach me what I need to know! [Socrates is slowly lowered earthwards.]

Socrates: What subject?

Strepsiades: Your course on public speaking and debating techniques. You see, my creditors have become absolutely ferocious. You should see how they're hounding me. What's more, Socrates, they're about to seize my belongings.

Socrates: How in the world could you fall so deeply in debt without realizing it?

Strepsiades: How? A great, greedy horsepox ate me up, that's how. But that's why I want instruction in your second Logic, you know the one—the get-away-without-paying argument. I'll pay you any price you ask. I swear it. By the gods.

Socrates: By the gods? The gods, my dear simple fellow, are a mere expression coined by vulgar superstition. We frown upon such coinage here.

## Discussing the Reading

1. What attitudes did Aristophanes attribute to Socrates?

2. In the *Dialogues* of his disciple Plato, Socrates was presented as a hero. Is this the way he appears in *The Clouds*?

3. Does education guarantee success? Explain.

**CRITICAL THINKING**
**Identifying Assumptions**

What do you think was Aristophanes' view of the value of education?

# Archimedes Destroys Roman Warships

**TIME FRAME**
*Late 3rd century* B.C.

**GEOGRAPHIC SETTING**
*Sicily*

The Greek physicist Archimedes [är′kə mē′dēz] (287?–212 B.C.) is one of the most famous Hellenistic scientists. Some of the anecdotes told about him suggest that he was much more interested in theoretical scientific ideas than in the practical world. However, Archimedes could also put his ideas to practical use. The following account by Plutarch describes how Archimedes protected his native city of Syracuse, on the island of Sicily, from a Roman naval attack for three years with elaborate defensive weaponry. Unfortunately, Syracuse did finally fall to the Roman armies in 212 B.C. and Archimedes was killed, supposedly while in his study, absorbed in a mathematical problem.

The king . . . perceiving the value of his arts, prevailed upon Archimedes to construct for him a number of machines, some for the attack and 5 some for the defense of a city, of which he [Archimedes] himself did not make use, as he spent most of his life in unwarlike and literary leisure, but now these engines were ready for use in Syr-10 acuse, and the inventor also was present to direct their working.

So when the Romans attacked by sea and land at once, the Syracusans were at first terrified and silent, dreading that 15 nothing could resist such an armament.

"Don't disturb my circles," Archimedes was traditionally supposed to have said to the soldier sent to bring the old mathematician to the Roman general Marcellus after the fall of Syracuse. Despite Marcellus's order that Archimedes was to be spared, the impatient soldier immediately killed him. The scene is depicted in a Roman mosaic from the 3rd century A.D.

The painting on the left, by the Italian artist Domenico Fetti (1588–1623), shows Archimedes studying some mathematical figures. The drawing on the right, by the Italian artist and engineer Leonardo da Vinci (1452–1519), shows (on the left) a design for an Archimedean screw, a device, attributed to Archimedes, that is used for raising water.

But Archimedes opened fire from his machines, throwing upon the land forces all manner of darts and great stones, with an incredible noise and 20 violence, which no man could withstand; but those upon whom they fell were struck down in heaps, and their ranks thrown into confusion, while some of the ships were suddenly seized 25 by iron hooks, and by a counter-balancing weight were drawn up and then plunged to the bottom. Others they caught by irons like hands or claws suspended from cranes, and first pulled 30 them up by their bows till they stood upright upon their sterns, and then cast down into the water, or by means of windlasses and tackles worked inside the city, dashed them against the cliffs 35 and rocks at the base of the walls, with terrible destruction to their crews. Often was seen the fearful sight of a ship lifted out of the sea into the air, swaying and balancing about, until the men were all 40 thrown out or overwhelmed with stones from slings, when the empty vessel would either be dashed against the fortifications or dropped into the sea by the claws being let go. . . .

45 When [the Romans] attacked [at night], expecting that they would not be seen, they again encountered a storm of blows from stones which fell perpendicularly upon their heads and darts which 50 were poured from all parts of the wall. They were forced to retire, and when they came within range of the larger machines, missiles were showered upon them as they retreated, destroying 55 many men and throwing the ships into great disorder, without their being able to retaliate. For most of the engines on the walls had been devised by Archimedes, and the Romans thought 60 that they were fighting against gods and not men, as destruction fell upon them from invisible hands. . . .

Yet Archimedes had so great a mind and such immense philosophic specu- 65 lations that although by inventing these engines he had acquired the glory of a more than human intellect, he would not condescend to leave behind him any writings upon the subject, 70 regarding the whole business of

mechanics and the useful arts as base and vulgar, but placed his whole study and delight in those speculations in which absolute beauty and excellence
75 appear unhampered by the necessities of life. . . .

### Discussing the Reading

1. Do you find this account of Archimedes' machines believable?

2. If Archimedes were alive today, would he be willing to participate in the development of the Strategic Defense Initiative (the project to develop a space-based missile-defense system for the United States)?

**CRITICAL THINKING**
**Recognizing Values**

Which is more important, theoretical or applied science? Support your view with examples.

# The Assassination of Julius Caesar

6A

**TIME FRAME**
*Mid-1st century* B.C.

**GEOGRAPHIC SETTING**
*Rome*

In 49 B.C. the Roman general Julius Caesar, with the backing of his loyal army fresh from a successful military campaign in Gaul (a region largely occupied by modern France), forced the Roman Senate to accept him as dictator for life. As a ruler he introduced many reforms that made him popular with the people. However, the Senate feared that Caesar meant to make himself king and establish a dynasty, a change in government that would threaten the Senate's role in the selection of Rome's rulers. A group of men including Marcus Brutus, one of his best friends, joined in a plot to murder Caesar. The following is Plutarch's description of how on March 15, 44 B.C., a day known to Romans as the "Ides of March," the assassination was carried out.

When Caesar entered, the Senate rose to do him honor, and some of the party of Brutus stood around his chair at the back, and others presented
5 themselves before him, as if their purpose was to support the prayer of Tillius Cimber [til′lyəs sim′bər] on behalf of his exiled brother, and they all joined in entreaty, following Caesar as far as his
10 seat. When he had taken his seat and was rejecting their entreaties, and, as they urged them still more strongly, began to show displeasure towards them individually, Tillius taking hold of
15 [Caesar's] toga with both his hands pulled it downwards from the neck,

"The Death of Caesar"
was painted in 1859 by
the French realist
Jean-Léon Gérome
(1824–1904).

which was the signal for the attack.
Casca was the first to strike him on the
neck with his sword, a blow neither
20 mortal nor severe, for as was natural at
the beginning of so bold a deed he was
confused, and Caesar turning round
seized the dagger and held it fast. And it
happened that at the same moment he
25 who was struck cried out in the Roman
language, "You villain, Casca, what are
you doing?" and he who had given the
blow cried out to his brother in Greek,
"Brother, help." Such being the begin-
30 ning, those who were not privy to the
conspiracy were prevented by conster-
nation and horror at what was going on
either from flying or going to aid, and
they did not even venture to utter a
35 word. And now each of the conspirators
bared his sword, and Caesar, being
hemmed in all round, in whatever direction he turned meeting blows and
swords aimed against his eyes and face,
40 driven about like a wild beast, was
caught in the hands of his enemies; for it
was arranged that all of them should
take a part in and taste of the deed of
blood. Accordingly Brutus also gave
45 him one blow in the groin. It is said by
some authorities, that he [Caesar]
defended himself against the rest,
moving about his body hither and
thither and calling out, till he saw that
50 Brutus had drawn his sword, when he
pulled his toga over his face and offered
no further resistance, having been
driven either by chance or by the conspirators to the base on which the statue
55 of Pompeius [pom′pē əs; Caesar's
defeated political rival] stood. And the
base was drenched with blood, as if
Pompeius was directing the vengeance

21

upon his enemy who was stretched
60 beneath his feet and writhing under his
many wounds; for he is said to have
received three and twenty wounds.
Many of the conspirators were
wounded by one another, while they
65 were aiming so many blows against one
body.

After Caesar was killed, though
Brutus came forward as if he was going
to say something about the deed, the
70 Senators, without waiting to listen,
rushed through the door and making
their escape filled the people with confusion and indescribable alarm, so that
some closed their houses, and others
75 left their tables and places of business,
and while some ran to the place to see
what had happened, others who had
seen it ran away. But Antonius
[an tō′nē əs] and Lepidus [lep′ə dəs],
80 who were the chief friends of Caesar,
stole away and fled for refuge to the
houses of other persons. The partisans
of Brutus, just as they were, warm from
the slaughter, and showing their bare

85 swords, advanced all in a body from the
Senate house to the Capitol, not like
men who were flying, but exultant and
confident, calling the people to liberty
and joined by the nobles who met them.

# Roman Baths: Pro and Con

**TIME FRAME**
*1st-2nd century* A.D.

**GEOGRAPHIC SETTING**
*Rome*

Every Roman city had several bath-
houses. These public baths were often
large and beautiful buildings, multileveled
structures that included steam rooms,
bathing and swimming pools, gardens,
gyms, and libraries. The baths were
important centers of community and
social life, as well as athletic clubs.
Despite the cultural significance of the
public baths, opinion was divided over
their value. The authors of the following
two passages express quite different
views on the virtues of the baths. Lucian
[lü′shən] (c. A.D. 125–200) was a Greek
satirist; Seneca [sen′ə kə] (4? B.C.–A.D.
65) was a Roman philosopher.

On entering [a bathhouse], one is
received into a public hall of good
size, with ample accommodations for
servants and attendants. On the left are
5 the lounging rooms, also of just the
right sort for a bath, attractive, brightly
lighted retreats. Then, besides them, a
hall, larger than need be for the purposes of a bath, but necessary for the
10 reception of richer persons. Next,
[large] locker rooms to undress in, on
each side, with a very high and bril-
liantly lighted hall between them, in

which are three swimming pools of cold
water; it is finished in Laconian
[lā kō′nē ən] marble, and has two
statues of white marble in the ancient
style, one of Hygeia [hī jē′ə; goddess of
health], the other of Aesculapius
[es′kyə lā′pē əs; god of healing]. . . .

Then near this is another hall, the
most beautiful in the world, in which
one can stand or sit with comfort, linger
without danger, and stroll about with
profit. It also is [shining] with Phrygian
[frij′ē ən] marble clear to the roof. Next
comes the hot corridor, faced with
Numidian [nü mid′ē ən] marble. The
hall beyond it is very beautiful, full of
abundant light and aglow with color
like that of purple hangings. It contains
three hot tubs. . . . Why should I go on
to tell you of the exercising floor and the
cloak rooms? . . . Moreover, it is beauti-
fied with all other marks of thoughtful-

ness—with two toilets, many exits, and
two devices for telling time, a water
clock that makes a bellowing sound and
a sundial.

[Lucian, *Hippias, or the Bath*]

I live over a bathing establishment.
Picture to yourself now the assort-
ment of voices, the sound of which is
enough to sicken one. When the
stronger fellows are exercising and
swinging heavy leaden weights in their
hands, when they are working hard or
pretending to be working hard, I hear
their groans; and whenever they release
their pent-up breath, I hear their hissing
and jarring breathing. When I have to
do with a lazy fellow who is content
with a cheap rubdown, I hear the slap of
the hand pummeling his shoulders,

Below on the left is a mosaic from the Baths of Caracalla, which were completed in A.D. 217. This bull-necked gladiator suggests one of the athletes to whose noisy exertions Seneca was forced to listen. On the right are the ruins of a Roman bath in what is now Turkey. The floor of one of the pools is gone, revealing the supports below. Heated air, circulating among these supports, helped to warm the water in the pool.

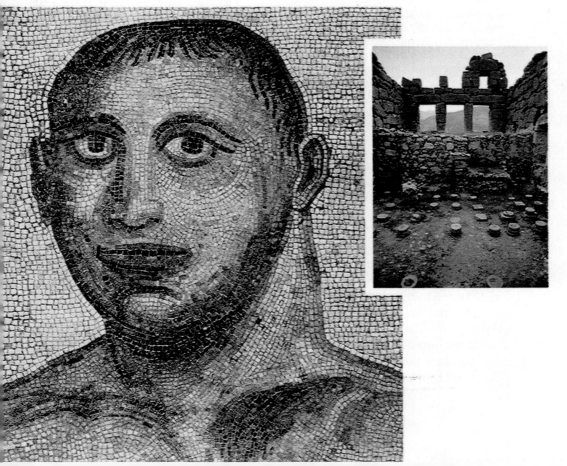

changing its sound according as the
hand is laid flat or curved. If now a
professional ball player comes along
and begins to keep score, I am done for.
Add to this the arrest of a brawler or a
20 thief, and the fellow who always likes to
hear his own voice in the bath, and
those who jump into the pool with a
mighty splash as they strike the
water. . . . It disgusts me to enumerate
25 the varied cries of the sausage dealer
and confectioner and of all the peddlers
of the cook shops, hawking their wares,
each with his own peculiar [cry].

[Seneca, *Moral Epistles*]

## Discussing the Reading

1. What is the origin and meaning of the word *hygiene*?

2. What other purposes did the Roman baths serve besides cleansing?

**CRITICAL THINKING**
**Making Inferences**

Lucian's and Seneca's contrasting views on the Roman baths offer suggestions about their respective personalities. Using this reading as a basis, make inferences about the characters of these two writers.

# A Hindu Warrior's Duty

**TIME FRAME**
*5th-4th century* B.C.

**GEOGRAPHIC SETTING**
*India*

The following is an excerpt from the *Bhagavad Gita* [bug′ə vəd gē′tä], or "Song of the Lord," a philosophical dialogue that forms part of *Mahabharata* [mä hä′bä′rə tä], a vast epic poem that was probably composed between 500 and 300 B.C. The central plot of the epic concerns a great struggle between two families of royal cousins for control of a kingdom in northern India. In the following scene, the two armies are facing each other in the final battle. The leader of one, Arjuna [är′jü nə], hesitates, fearing that to undertake the slaughter of his kinsmen for a worldly end must be sinful. The Hindu god Krishna [krish′nə], who is serving as Arjuna's charioteer, reassures him in the following words.

W hence this lifeless dejection, Arjuna, in this hour, the hour of trial? Strong men know not despair, Arjuna, for this wins neither heaven nor
5 earth.

Fall not into degrading weakness, for this becomes not a man who is a man. Throw off this ignoble discouragement, and arise like a fire that burns all before
10 it. . . .

Thy tears are for those beyond tears; and are thy words words of wisdom? The wise grieve not for those who live; and they grieve not for those who die—
15 for life and death shall pass away.

Because we all have been for all time: I, and thou, and those kings of men. And we all shall be for all time, we all for ever and ever.

20 As the Spirit of our mortal body wanders on in childhood, and youth and old age, the Spirit wanders on to a new body: of this the sage has no doubts.

From the world of the senses, Arjuna,
25 comes heat and comes cold, and pleasure and pain. They come and they go: they are transient. Arise above them, strong soul.

The man whom these cannot move,
30 whose soul is one, beyond pleasure and pain, is worthy of life in Eternity.

The unreal never is: the Real never is not. This truth indeed has been seen by those who can see the true.

This Sanskrit manuscript of the Indian epic poem the *Mahabharata* dates from 1841. Scenes from the life of the god Krishna are painted on the inside of the wooden covers. Krishna is the principal speaker in the *Bhagavad Gita*, the philosophical dialogue that is the most celebrated portion of the *Mahabharata*.

35 Interwoven in his creation, the Spirit is beyond destruction. No one can bring to an end the Spirit which is everlasting.

For beyond time he dwells in these bodies, though these bodies have an 40 end in their time; but he remains immeasurable, immortal. Therefore, great warrior, carry on thy fight.

If any man thinks he slays, and if another thinks he is slain, neither 45 knows the ways of truth. The Eternal in man cannot kill: the Eternal in man cannot die.

He is never born, and he never dies. He is in Eternity: he is for evermore. 50 Never-born and eternal, beyond times gone or to come, he does not die when the body dies.

When a man knows him as never-born, everlasting, never-changing, 55 beyond all destruction, how can that man kill a man, or cause another to kill?

As a man leaves an old garment and puts on one that is new, the Spirit leaves his mortal body and wanders on to one 60 that is new.

Weapons cannot hurt the Spirit and fire can never burn him. Untouched is he by drenching waters, untouched is he by parching winds.

65 Beyond the power of sword and fire, beyond the power of waters and winds, the Spirit is everlasting, omnipresent, never-changing, never-moving, ever One.

70 Invisible is he to mortal eyes, beyond thought and beyond change. Know that he is, and cease from sorrow.

But if he were born again and again, and again and again he were to die, even 75 then, victorious man, cease thou from sorrow.

For all things born in truth must die, and out of death in truth comes life. Face to face with what must be, cease 80 thou from sorrow.

Invisible before birth are all beings and after death invisible again. They are seen between two unseens. Why in this truth find sorrow?

85 One sees him in a vision of wonder, and another gives us words of his

wonder. There is one who hears of his wonder; but he hears and knows him not.

90 The Spirit that is in all beings is immortal in them all: for the death of what cannot die, cease thou to sorrow.

Think thou also of thy duty and do not waver. There is no greater good for a
95 warrior than to fight in righteous war.

There is a war that opens the doors of heaven, Arjuna! Happy the warriors whose fate is to fight such war.

But to forgo this fight for righteous-
100 ness is to forgo thy duty and honor: is to fall into transgression.

Men will tell of thy dishonor both now and in times to come. And to a man who is in honor, dishonor is more than
105 death.

The great warriors will say that thou hast run from the battle through fear; and those who thought great things of thee will speak of thee in scorn.

110 And thine enemies will speak of thee in contemptuous words of ill-will and derision, pouring scorn upon thy

courage. Can there be for a warrior a more shameful fate?

115 In death thy glory in heaven, in victory thy glory on earth. Arise therefore, Arjuna, with thy soul ready to fight.

Prepare for war with peace in thy soul. Be in peace in pleasure and pain,
120 in gain and in loss, in victory or in the loss of a battle. In this peace there is no sin.

## Discussing the Reading

1. Explain Krishna's argument that it is impossible to kill or be killed.

2. Why does Krishna feel that Arjuna must fight?

### CRITICAL THINKING
### Analyzing Comparisons

Do the comparisons made by Krishna in lines 20–23 and 57–60 show any reverence for the body as dwelling-place of the Spirit? Why or why not?

## A Buddhist Philosopher-King

7B

TIME FRAME
*3rd century* B.C.

GEOGRAPHIC SETTING
*India*

One of the world's great religions, Buddhism [bùd'iz əm] was founded in northern India in the 6th century B.C. Its most notable convert was Asoka [ə sō' kə], who in the 3rd century B.C. ruled an empire that included most of India. His first military campaign, against the Kalinga [kə ling'gə] people of southeastern India, was also his last. He was so horrified by the scale of the slaughter caused by his conquest of Kalinga that he resolved never again to resort to warfare. It was his ambition that his government should embody the Buddhist ideal of *dharma* [där'mə], "righteousness." He had his laws inscribed on rocks and pillars throughout his empire. The following are some of his edicts.

When [Asoka], Beloved of the Gods, [had ruled] eight years Kalinga was conquered. 150,000 people were deported, 100,000 were killed, and
5 many times that number died. But after the conquest of Kalinga, the Beloved of the Gods began to follow Righteousness, to love Righteousness, and to give instruction in Righteousness. Now the
10 Beloved of the Gods regrets the conquest of Kalinga, for when an independent country is conquered people are killed, they die, or are deported, and that the Beloved of the Gods finds very
15 painful and grievous. . . .

This sculpture of a seated Buddha, which dates from the 2nd or 3rd century A.D., is in the Greek-inspired Gandharan [gan dä'-rən] style of Indian art. This Greek influence may have reached India as a result of contact with the kingdom established by Alexander the Great in Bactria, a country northwest of India, or through trade with the Roman empire.

I have had this inscription of Righteousness engraved that all my sons and grandsons may not seek to gain new victories, that in whatever victories they
20 may gain they may prefer forgiveness and light punishment that they may consider the only [valid] victory the victory of Righteousness, which is of value both in this world and the next, and that
25 all their pleasure may be in Righteousness.

[from the 13th Rock Edict]

Here no animal is to be killed for sacrifice, and no festivals are to be held, . . . Formerly in the Beloved of the God's kitchen several hundred thousand animals were killed daily for food; but now at the time of writing only three are killed—two peacocks and a deer, [and the deer is not slaughtered regularly]. Even these three animals will not be killed in future.

[from the 1st Pillar Edict]

Everywhere in the empire of the Beloved of the Gods, and even beyond his frontiers . . . the Beloved of the Gods has provided medicines for man and beast. Wherever medicinal plants have not been found they have been sent there and planted. Roots and fruits have also been sent where they did not grow, and have been planted. Wells have been dug along the roads for the use of man and beast.

[from the 2nd Rock Edict]

By order of the Beloved of the Gods. Addressed to the officers in charge of Tosali [tō säl'ē; a city in Kalinga]. . . . Often a man is imprisoned and tortured unjustly, and then he is liberated for no [apparent] reason. Many other people suffer also [as a result of this injustice]. Therefore it is desirable that you should practice impartiality, but it cannot be attained if you are inclined to habits of jealousy, irritability, harshness, hastiness, [stubbornness], laziness, or [fatigue]. . . . This inscription has been engraved in order that the officials of the city should always see to it that no one is ever imprisoned or tortured without good cause. To ensure this I shall send out every five years on a tour of inspection officers who are not fierce or harsh.

[from 1st Separate Kalinga Edict]

King [Asoka] honors men of all faiths, members of religious orders and laymen alike, with gifts and various marks of esteem. Yet he does not value either gifts or honors as much as growth in the qualities essential to religion in men of all faiths.

This growth may take many forms, but its root is in guarding one's speech to avoid [praising] one's own faith and [condemning] the faith of others improperly or, when the occasion is appropriate, immoderately.

The faiths of others all deserve to be honored for one reason or another. By honoring them, one exalts one's own faith and at the same time performs a service to the faith of others. By acting otherwise, one injures one's own faith and also does disservice to that of others. For if a man [praises] his own faith and [condemns] another because of devotion to his own and because he wants to glorify it, he seriously injures his own faith.

[from the 12th Rock Edict]

## Discussing the Reading

1. In the *Bhagavad Gita* (see Reading 7A, lines 94–95), Krishna says, "There is no greater good for a warrior than to fight in righteous war." Would Asoka agree or disagree with this view? Explain your answer.

2. If Asoka were alive today, with what kinds of causes would he identify himself?

**CRITICAL THINKING**
**Recognizing Values**

Do you agree with Asoka's assertion that if people praise their own religious beliefs and condemn the beliefs of others, they injure both faiths? Is this expecting too much of people's capacity for tolerance?

# The Riddles of Taoism

**TIME FRAME**
*4th century* B.C.

**GEOGRAPHIC SETTING**
*China*

The image below, a detail of a painting by Ch'en Hung-shou (1598–1652), recalls Chuang Tzu's famous dream that he was "a butterfly fluttering about, enjoying itself."

Taoism [dou'iz'əm] was the second most important philosophy produced by Zhou [jō] China (1027–256 B.C.), second only to Confucianism. The name *taoism* refers to the central subject of this philosophy, the *tao* (dou), or "way," the cosmic order that makes all things what they are but is utterly hidden and unknowable. Many scholars see Taoism, which emphasized nature, harmony, individual differences, and tolerance, as complementary to the strict, rigorous, traditional morality of Confucianism. Taoism's teachings are recorded in two books, one attributed to Laozi [lou'dzŭ'] (604?–529? B.C.), the traditional founder of the philosophy, and the other to a disciple of his, Chuang Tzu [jwäng' dzŭ'] (c.365–c.290 B.C.). Both books taught lessons through parables, anecdotes, and witty riddles, as the following selections from the *Chuang Tzu* show.

Once upon a time, Chuang Chou [jwäng' jō'; i.e., Chuang Tzu] dreamed that he was a butterfly, a butterfly fluttering about, enjoying itself. It did not know that it was Chuang Chou. Suddenly he awoke with a start and he was Chuang Chou again. But he did not know whether he was Chuang Chou who had dreamed that he was a butterfly, or whether he was a butterfly dreaming that he was Chuang Chou. Between Chuang Chou and the butterfly there must be some distinction. This is what is called the transformation of things.

From the point of preference, if we approve of anyone who is approved of by someone [at least himself], then there is no one who may not be approved of. If we condemn anyone who is condemned by someone else, then there is no one who may not be condemned. To know that Yao [you; a traditional sage-king] and Chieh [jē'ye; a tyrant] would each approve of himself and condemn the other, then we have a clear realization of human preference. . . .

A battering-ram can knock down a city wall, but it cannot stop a hole—the uses of different implements are different. The horses Ch'i-chi [chē'jē'] and Hua-liu [hwa'lyü'] could gallop a thousand *li* [lē; a *li* is approximately one-third of a mile] in one day, but for catching rats they were not equal to a wild cat or a weasel—the gifts of different creatures are different. An owl can catch fleas at night, and see the tip of a hair, but if it comes out in the daytime it may stare with its eyes and not see a mountain—the natures of different creatures are different.

29

Once Chuang Tzu was fishing in the P'u [bü] River when the King of Ch'u [chü] sent two of his ministers to announce that he wished to entrust to
5 Chuang Tzu the care of his entire domain.

Chuang Tzu held his fishing pole and, without turning his head, said: "I have heard that Ch'u possesses a sacred tor-
10 toise which has been dead for three thousand years and which the king keeps wrapped up in a box and stored in his ancestral temple. Is this tortoise better off dead and with its bones vener-
15 ated, or would it be better off alive with its tail dragging in the mud?"

"It would be better off alive and dragging its tail in the mud," the two ministers replied.
20 "Then go away!" said Chuang Tzu, "and I will drag my tail in the mud!"

## Discussing the Reading

1. Have you ever had the experience of being unable to distinguish between dream and reality? Did it alter your feelings about life to any degree? Explain.

2. In the second passage, does Chuang Tzu seem to mean that a moral difference (like that between Yao and Chieh) is equivalent to a physical difference (like that between a horse and a weasel)? Why or why not?

**CRITICAL THINKING**
**Making Generalizations**

Using the third passage as evidence, make a generalization about the Taoist attitude toward ambition.

# Civil Service Examinations in Tang China

8B

**TIME FRAME**
*Late 8th century* A.D.

**GEOGRAPHIC SETTING**
*China*

The golden age of Chinese poetry was the period of the Tang [täng] dynasty (618–907). Bai Juyi [bī' jü'ē] (772–846), also called Po Chü-i [bō' jü'ē], was the best known of the later Tang poets. His clear poetic style, his avoidance of learned allusions and ambiguities, earned him during his lifetime a unique popularity among his contemporaries of all classes. His father's death in 794 left Bai Juyi's family in difficult circumstances, and it was not until the poet was 28 years old that he set out for the imperial capital to take the examinations for government service. These examinations were intended to ensure that literate and intelligent people were recruited for service in the imperial administration. The examinations were written tests that were given once every three years. They covered current events, Confucian classics, creative writing, Chinese law, and

mathematics. While taking the test, each candidate sat in a small, separate room that was somewhat like a telephone booth. In some towns acres of these booths sat in long rows. The test lasted three days, during which time food was brought in by servants, and officials watched from high towers to see that no one cheated. Bai Juyi had to do well on these examinations if he was to have an official career and recognition as a scholar. In the last poem he wrote before taking the examinations, Bai Juyi reflects on his loneliness (as a provincial in the capital) and the passing of youth (at 28 he was older than most candidates).

The awninged coaches, the singing and the flutes fill the City with their din;

Below at the left is a portrait of Bai Juyi. On the right is a painting that depicts an examination for the imperial civil service being given in Tang China. The emperor is shown overseeing the examination from the pavilion at the rear, while candidates such as Bai Juyi demonstrated knowledge of Confucian texts in order to be eligible for government service.

One there is, in the midst of them all,
5 who "stands facing the corner."
Sad at midnight when he draws the
    blind and moonbeams fill the room,
Weeping at dusk when the green hills
    make him think of home.
10 The spring wind blows the fields, new
    buds break;
The light yellow of the willow branches
    is wet with a sprinkling of rain.
My youth is gone, I am almost thirty
15    and know that I have missed
My last chance in this life to be young
    and happy in the spring.

Bai Juyi passed his exam with first-class honors, but it took him some time to believe that with his "mean and humble origin" he could deserve such good fortune. On the tenth day after the results came out he wrote the following.

I swear that till my dying day I will continue to repay what my lord has done for me, and repay him in this sense: that I will strive to do only what
5 he would wish, that I will further his plans. . . . I must make all my actions conform to a strict standard and all my

writings must inculcate the highest
principles. I must make a practice of
10 studying at set times and never be idle
or put study aside. As to advancement
in the world, I must let it come at its own
pace and not go out of my way. . . . I
have obtained a First Class in the exami-
15 nation and have in so doing made a
name for myself; but that is no reason to
be puffed up or self-satisfied.

A few weeks later Bai Juyi set out for
his home. In his poem "Parting from my
fellow-candidates . . . " he is finally able
to rejoice in the success he has had and
the future of a good career that lies
ahead.

---

F or ten years I never left my books;
I went up . . . and won unmerited
praise.
My high place I do not much prize;
5 The joy of my parents will first make
me proud.
Fellow students, six or seven men,
See me off as I leave the City gate.
My covered coach is ready to drive
10 away;
Flutes and strings blend their parting
tune.

Hopes achieved dull the pains of
parting,
15 Fumes of wine shorten the long
road . . .
Shod with wings is the horse of him
who rides
On a Spring day the road that leads to
20 home.

# Two Traditional African Occupations

**TIME FRAME**
*20th century*

**GEOGRAPHIC SETTING**
*Central and southern
Africa*

Bouba [bü′bə], a young herdsman from
Cameroon [kam′ə rün′], a country in
west central Africa, wrote the following
statement of his goals in a letter to his
pen pal in southern France in the 1950s.
It surely is representative of the dreams
of African pastoralists for thousands of
years.

**Letter from Bouba**

---

W hen I grow up I shall raise cows,
sheep, and goats. I won't grow
any crops, but with the milk from my

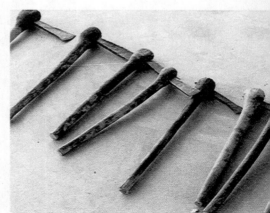

Below on the left are iron tools cast by a present-day blacksmith from the Ivory Coast, a country in West Africa. On the right are two wooden pulleys, also from the Ivory Coast, that have been ornamented with carvings of a woman and a cow.

cows I shall buy a big gourd of millet [grain].

With the meat of a goat or a ram killed each month we shall eat well.

Clothes will be no problem. I shall take a six-year-old bull to market and with what it brings I shall buy fine clothes.

My son will guard my sheep, my daughter will look after the goats, and I shall take the cows out to the pasture. There I may have to endure rain and storms, but the delicious, creamy milk will soon make me forget these discomforts.

When I grow old I shall employ paid shepherds. In the shadow of the "danki" [shade tree] I shall stretch myself on my sleeping mat, a glass of coffee by my side. "Bouba has more than a hundred head of livestock; he is one of the richest among us," the villagers will say.

When I am 80 years old I shall sell some of my animals and I shall spend the money on a pilgrimage to Mecca.

[signed] Bouba

The following is a traditional song from Zimbabwe [zim bä'bwe], a country in southeastern Africa. It celebrates a profession that, like the pastoralist's, is thousands of years old.

**In Praise of the Ironsmith**

Today this place is full of noise and jollity.
The guiding spirit that enables my
   husband to forge makes him do
   wonders.
All those who lack hoes for weeding,
   come and buy!

Hoes and choppers are here in plenty.
My husband is a craftsman in iron,
10 Truly a wizard at forging hoes.
Ah, here they are! they have come eager
    to find hoes.
Ah, the iron itself is aglow, it is molten
    red with heat,
15 And the ore is ruddy and incandescent.
My husband is an expert in working
    iron,
A craftsman who sticks like wax to his
    trade.
20 On the day when the urge to forge
    comes upon him,
The bellows do everything but speak.
The pile of slag rises higher and higher.
Just look at what has been forged,
25 At the choppers, at the hoes, at the
    battle axes,
And here at the pile of hatchets, large
    and small.
Then look at the double-bladed knives
30  and adzes.
Merely to list them all seems like
    boasting.
As for fowls and goats, they cover my
    yard.

35 They all come from the sale of tools and
    weapons.
Here is where you see me eating at ease
    with a spoon.

## Discussing the Reading

1. Bouba has planned out his whole life, right up to the religious pilgrimage to Mecca that, like a good Muslim, he will take in his old age. Compare your ambitions to his. How has society determined your definition of success?

2. How does the wife in Zimbabwe achieve success? What does this indicate about a woman's place in this society?

**CRITICAL THINKING**
**Predicting Effects**

Bouba indicates that success for him would be owning more than a hundred head of livestock. If many other young people in Bouba's community had the same ambition, what might be the effects on the economy and environment of the area?

# Mayan Splendor

**TIME FRAME**
*14th–15th centuries*
**GEOGRAPHIC SETTING**
*Central America*

The ancient Mayan [mī′ən] people developed a form of writing with which they recorded their calendars, religious rituals, and some history. They wrote in books called codices [kō′də sēz′; singular *codex*], but because the Spanish conquerors early in the 16th century destroyed any of these books that they found, only four codices are known to exist today and scholars disagree on how to translate them. Shortly after the Spanish conquest, however, some Mayan priests learned the Spanish alphabet and copied some codices, writing the Mayan words but using Spanish letters. The most famous of these books to survive is

the *Popol Vuh* [pō pül′ vü′] or "Council Book," telling the creation myths and history of the Quiché [kē′chā′] tribe of southern Guatemala. The following selection from the *Popol Vuh* describes the period—the 14th and 15th centuries—when the Quiché reached the height of their power.

And then they got up and came to the citadel of Rotten Cane . . . And they built many houses there. And they also built houses for the gods, putting
5 these in the center of the highest part of the citadel. They came and they stayed.

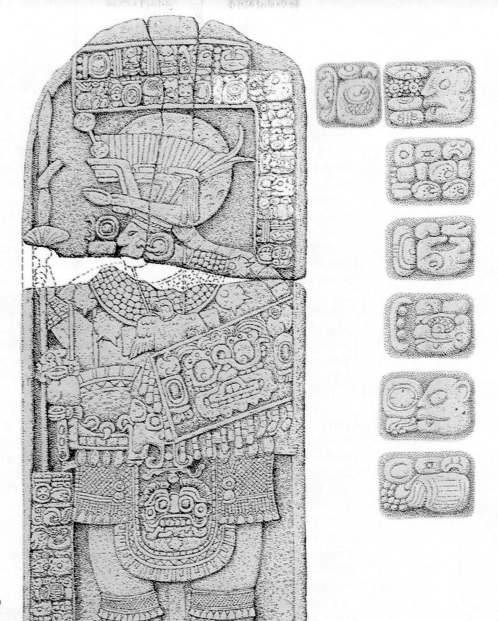

On the left is a drawing of a Mayan stela [stē′-lə], an upright stone slab ornamented with carving. The standing figure is a Mayan ruler dressed to perform a sacrifice. The person to be sacrificed is shown beneath the ruler's feet. On the right is a detail from the upper right portion of the stela, showing individual glyphs [glifs], or pictographic symbols.

After that their domain grew larger; they were more numerous and more crowded. Again they planned their great houses, which had to be regrouped and sorted out . . . Then splendor and majesty grew among the Quiché. The greatness and weight of the Quiché reached its full splendor and majesty with the surfacing and plastering of the canyon and citadel. The tribes came, whether small or great and whatever the titles of their lords, adding to the greatness of the Quiché. As splendor and majesty grew, so grew the houses of gods and the houses of lords.

But the lords could not have accomplished it, they could not have done the work of building their houses or the houses of the gods, were it not for the fact that their vassals had become numerous. They neither had to lure them nor did they kidnap them or take them away by force, because each one of them rightfully belonged to the lords. And the elder and younger brothers of the lords also became populous. Each lord led a crowded life, crowded with petitions. The lords were truly valued and had truly great respect. . . .

They were great lords, they were people of genius. Plumed Serpent and Cotuha [kō tü ä'] were lords of genius, and Quicab [kwē cäb'] and Cauizimah [kä ü ē zē mä'] were lords of genius. They knew whether war would occur; everything they saw was clear to them. Whether there would be death, or whether there would be famine, or whether quarrels would occur, they knew it for certain, since there was a place to see it, there was a book. Council Book was their name for it.

But it wasn't only in this way that they were lords. They were great in their own being and observed great fasts. As a way of cherishing their buildings and cherishing their lordship, they fasted for long periods, they did penance before their gods. . . . For nine score days they would fast, and for nine they would do penance and burn offerings. . . . They just stayed in the houses of the gods, each day. All they did was keep the days, burn offerings, and do penance. They were there whether it was dark or dawn; they just cried their hearts and their guts out when they asked for light and life for their vassals and their domain. . . .

And it wasn't merely that they crushed the canyons and citadels of the tribes, whether small or great, but that the tribes paid a great price: There came turquoise, there came metal. And there came drops of jade and other gems that measured the width of four fingers or a full fist across. And there came green and red featherwork, the tribute of all the tribes. . . .

And the lords had undergone pain and withstood it; their rise to splendor had not been sudden. . . .

This is enough about the being of Quiché given that there is no longer a place to see it. There is the original book and ancient writing owned by the lords, now lost, but even so, everything has been completed here concerning Quiché which is now named Santa Cruz.

## Discussing the Reading

1. What role did religion play in Mayan society? Support your answer.

2. What was expected of the rulers of Mayan society? What did they receive in return?

### CRITICAL THINKING
**Making Generalizations**

The Mayan rulers performed important religious roles. What should be the relationship between political leaders and organized religion today?

Torn by lions, St. Ignatius, bishop of Antioch in the 2nd century, is shown in this detail from an illustration in a medieval service book used in the Eastern Orthodox Church. St. Ignatius was the first Christian to be martyred in the Colosseum at Rome.

# Christian Martyrs

**TIME FRAME**
*Late 2nd century* A.D.

**GEOGRAPHIC SETTING**
*France*

Romans were generally very tolerant of all religions in their empire. As the historian Gibbon observes, "The various modes of worship which prevailed in the Roman world were all considered by the people as equally true, by the philosopher as equally false, and by the magistrate as equally useful." Nevertheless, these same magistrates could be quite harsh to peoples who refused to participate in the patriotic ceremonies which Christians and Jews called "emperor worship," but exceptions even for this could be made. While in the early centuries Christianity spread without any systematic government opposition, there were periodic outbreaks of persecution. In A.D. 177, according to one historian of the early church, "an ugly persecution broke out with savage violence against Christians at Lyons and Vienne in [south-central France]; the emperor Marcus Aurelius [mär′kəs  ô rē′lē əs] (A.D. 121–180) had directed that they should be tortured to death, and no refinement of cruelty was spared." The bravery of the Christian martyrs, however, was recorded by several witnesses. Early in the 4th century, the Christian bishop and historian Eusebius [yü sē′bē əs] (A.D. 260?–340?) wrote the following account.

There were also arrested certain heathen slaves of our members, since the governor had publicly commanded that we should all be prose-
5 cuted, and these by the snare of Satan, fearing the tortures which they saw the saints suffering, when the soldiers urged them, falsely accused us

37

of . . . things which it is not right for us either to speak of or to think of or even to believe that such things could ever happen among men [probably cannibalism based on a literal reading of the Lord's Supper]. When this rumor spread all men turned like beasts against us, so that even if any had formerly been lenient for friendship's sake they then became furious and raged against us, and there was fulfilled that which was spoken by our Lord that "the time will come when whosoever killeth you will think that he doeth God service."

Maturus and Sanctus and Blandina and Attalus were led forth to the wild beasts, to the public, and to a common exhibition of the inhumanity of the heathen, for the day of fighting with beasts was specially appointed for the Christians. Maturus and Sanctus passed again through all torture in the amphitheater as though they had suffered nothing before, but rather as though, having conquered the opponent in many bouts, they were now striving for his crown. Once more they ran the gauntlet in the accustomed manner, endured the worrying of the wild beasts, and everything which the maddened public, some in one way, some in another, were howling for and commanding, finally, the iron chair on which the roasting of their own bodies clothed them with its reek. Their persecutors did not stop even here, but went on growing more and more furious, wishing to conquer their endurance, yet gained nothing from Sanctus beyond the sound of the [Christian] confession which he had been accustomed to make from the beginning.

. . . but Blandina was hung on a stake and offered as a prey to the wild beasts that were let in. She seemed to be hanging in the shape of a cross, and by her continuous prayer gave great zeal to the combatants, while they looked on during the contest, and with their outward eyes saw in the form of their sister him who was crucified for them, to persuade those who believe on him that all who suffer for the glory of Christ have for ever fellowship with the living God. Then when none of the beasts would touch her she was taken down from the stake and brought back into the jail, and was thus preserved for another contest. . . .

In addition to all this, on the last day of the gladiatorial sports, Blandina was again brought in with Ponticus, a boy of about fifteen years old, and they had been brought in every day to see the torture of the others, and efforts were made to force them to swear by the idols, and the mob was furious against them because they had remained steadfast and disregarded them, so that there was neither pity for the youth of the boy nor respect for the sex of the woman. They exposed them to all the terrors and put them through every torture in turn, trying to make them swear, but not being able to do so. For Ponticus was encouraged by the Christian sister, so that even the heathen saw that she was exhorting and strengthening him, and after nobly enduring every torture he gave up his spirit. But the blessed Blandina, last of all, like a noble mother who had encouraged her children and sent them forth triumphant to the king, having herself endured all the tortures of the children, hastened to them, rejoicing and glad at her departure as though invited to a marriage feast rather than cast to the beasts. And after scourging, after the beasts, after the gridiron, she was at last put in a net and thrown to a bull. . . . And so she too was sacrificed, and the heathen themselves confessed that never before among them had a woman suffered so much and so long.

## Discussing the Reading

1. Why were the Christians at Lyons and Vienne persecuted?

2. Like Asoka (see Reading 7B), Marcus Aurelius was a philosopher who attempted to rule his empire wisely and justly. Nevertheless, he also vigorously persecuted the Christians. What reasons might he have had for pursuing this policy?

**CRITICAL THINKING**
**Identifying Assumptions**

What does Eusebius's use of the word *martyr* in his account of the persecution of the Christians indicate about his point of view? How might the Romans present at the amphitheater have described the Christians?

# A Profile of Charlemagne

# 10B

**TIME FRAME**
*Early 9th century* A.D.

**GEOGRAPHIC SETTING**
*Western Europe*

"Of all kings Charlemagne was the most eager in his search for wise men," observes the Prologue of Einhard's short biography of him. Einhard [īn'härt] (770–840) himself was one of these scholars with whom Charlemagne (742–814) surrounded himself. Educated in a monastery and then sent to Charlemagne's palace school at Aachen [ä'kən], Einhard became the king's secretary, adviser, and friend. The following excerpt is from his brief account of "the life and day-to-day habits of Charlemagne, my lord and patron," which Einhard wrote between 829 and 836, some years after the king's death.

T he Emperor was strong and well built. He was tall in stature, but not excessively so, for his height was just

Emperor Charlemagne is pictured on the left in this page from an illuminated manuscript. On the right appears Pepin, the second of Charlemagne's three sons by his second wife. Before his early death, Pepin was made King of Italy by his father.

seven times the length of his own feet. The top of his head was round, and his eyes were piercing and unusually large. His nose was slightly longer than normal, he had a fine head of white hair and his expression was gay and good-humored. . . .

He spent much of his time on horseback and out hunting, which came naturally to him, for it would be difficult to find another race on earth who could equal the Franks in this activity. He took delight in steam baths at the thermal springs, and loved to exercise himself in the water whenever he could. He was an extremely strong swimmer and in this sport no one could surpass him. . . .

He was moderate in his eating and drinking and especially so in drinking; for he hated to see drunkenness in any man, and even more so in himself and his friends. All the same, he could not go long without food, and he often used to complain that fasting made him feel ill. . . . His main meal of the day was served in four courses, in addition to the roast meat which his hunters used to bring in on spits and which he enjoyed more than any other food. During his meal he would listen to a public reading or some other entertainment. Stories would be recited for him, or the doing of the ancients told again. He took great pleasure in the books of Saint Augustine. . . .

He spoke easily and fluently, and could express with great clarity whatever he had to say. He was not content with his mother tongue, but took the trouble to learn foreign languages. He learnt Latin so well that he spoke it as fluently as his own tongue; but he understood Greek better than he could speak it. He was eloquent to the point of sometimes seeming almost garrulous.

He paid the greatest attention to the liberal arts; and he had a great respect for men who taught them, bestowing high honors upon them. . . . The Emperor spent much time and effort in studying rhetoric, dialectic, and especially astrology. He applied himself to mathematics and traced the course of the stars with great attention and care. He also tried to learn to write. With this object in view he used to keep writing-tablets and notebooks under the pillows on his bed, so that he could try his hand at forming letters during his leisure moments; but although he tried very hard, he had begun too late in life and he made little progress. . . .

Charlemagne was determined to give his children, his daughters just as much as his sons, a proper training in the liberal arts which had formed the subject of his own studies. . . . These girls were extraordinarily beautiful and greatly loved by their father. It is a remarkable fact that, as a result of this, he kept them with him in his household until the very day of his death, instead of giving them in marriage to his own men or to foreigners, maintaining that he could not live without them.

Wearing his tiara, or triple crown, Pope Leo III is shown crowning Charlemagne as Holy Roman Emperor in the medieval painting on the opposite page. The ceremony took place at St. Peter's Basilica in Rome on Christmas Day in the year 800.

## Discussing the Reading

1. What qualities and skills of leadership were attributed to Charlemagne by Einhard? Which of these characteristics would be needed to be President of the United States?

2. What might have been the author's motives for creating such an attractive picture of Charlemagne?

### CRITICAL THINKING
### Making Decisions

Assume that Lycurgus, Alexander, Asoka (see Readings 4A, 4B, and 7B), and Charlemagne are all available to rule the area where you live. Whom would you choose as your leader? Give your reasons.

This illustration from a 14th-century French manuscript shows both the capture of Jerusalem by the Crusaders and scenes from the life of Christ. In the center of the picture, the Crusaders are storming the walls of the city; at the bottom right, the artillery is firing rocks; in the upper portion, the trial, death, and burial of Jesus are depicted on the windows.

# The Crusaders Capture Jerusalem

11A

**TIME FRAME**

*Late 11th century*

**GEOGRAPHIC SETTING**

*Palestine*

The only Crusade that achieved significant military success was the first one (1096–1099), which, as one historian observes, "took the Muslim world completely by surprise and found it in a state of political disunity that obstructed the speed and efficiency of its preparations for war." Led by French princes and nobles, the army of the First Crusade included 3,000 knights on horseback and 12,000 foot soldiers. In 1099 this army fought its way from Constantinople into Jerusalem and mercilessly slaughtered Muslim, Jewish, and even Christian residents. The following is a description of

the conquest of Jerusalem written at the time by an anonymous Christian chronicler. *Saracens* (sar'ə sənz) was the general term used by the Crusaders for the various Muslim peoples they encountered.

D uring this siege [of Jerusalem], we suffered so badly from thirst that we sewed up the skins of oxen and buffaloes, and we used to carry water in
5 them for the distance of nearly six miles. We drank the water from these vessels, although it stank, and what

with foul water and barley bread we suffered great distress and affliction every day, for the Saracens used to lie in wait for our men by every spring and pool, where they killed them and cut them to pieces; moreover they used to carry off [the Crusaders' horses] into their caves and secret places in the rocks.

Our leaders then decided to attack the city with [battering rams and siege towers], so that we might enter it and worship at our Savior's Sepulcher. . . . All this time we were suffering so badly from the shortage of water that for one penny a man could not buy sufficient to quench his thirst.

On Wednesday and Thursday we launched a fierce attack upon the city, both by day and by night, from all sides, but before we attacked our bishops and priests preached to us, and told us to go in procession round Jerusalem to the glory of God, and to pray and give alms and fast, as faithful men should do. On Friday at dawn we attacked the city from all sides but could achieve nothing, so that we were all astounded and very much afraid, yet, when that hour came when our Lord Jesus Christ deigned to suffer for us upon the cross, our knights were fighting bravely on the siege-tower, led by Duke Godfrey and Count Eustace his brother. At that moment one of our knights, called Lethold, succeeded in getting on to the wall. As soon as he reached it, all the defenders fled along the walls and through the city, and our men went after them, killing them and cutting them down as far as Solomon's Temple, where there was such a massacre that our men were wading up to their ankles in enemy blood.

. . . So our men entered the city, chasing the Saracens and killing them up to Solomon's Temple, where they took refuge and fought hard against our men for the whole day, so that all the temple was streaming with their blood. At last, when the pagans were defeated, our men took many prisoners, both men and women, in the temple. They killed whom they chose, and whom they chose they saved alive. On the roof of the Temple of Solomon were crowded great numbers of pagans of both sexes, to whom Tancred and Gaston of Bearn gave their banners.

After this our men rushed round the whole city, seizing gold and silver, horses and mules, and houses full of all sorts of goods, and they all came rejoicing and weeping from excess of gladness to worship at the Sepulcher of our Savior Jesus, and there they fulfilled their vows to him. Next morning they went cautiously up on to the Temple roof and attacked the Saracens, both men and women, cutting off their heads with drawn swords.

## Discussing the Reading

1. Besides the lack of water, what other problems would the Crusaders have faced in fighting in the Middle East?

2. After such a long siege, why were the Crusaders suddenly successful in taking Jerusalem in just three days?

3. The Christian chronicler referred to the Muslim defenders of Jerusalem killed by the Crusaders as *Saracens* and *pagans*. Keeping in mind that Jerusalem was a city sacred to Islam as well as Christianity, how might a Muslim chronicler have referred to these same defenders?

### CRITICAL THINKING
### Predicting Effects

Given the ferocity of the Crusaders' conduct in their conquest of Jerusalem, what were the likely consequences of this victory?

# The Church Encounters the New Learning

**TIME FRAME**
*Early 12th century*

**GEOGRAPHIC SETTING**
*France*

During the 1100s, when universities started all over Christendom and learning grew, one of the most popular and eager scholars was Pierre Abelard [ab′ə lärd] (1079–1142). He began to question everything, even Church doctrine, as the selection below from his famous book *Sic et Non (Yes and No)* shows. The rediscovery by European thinkers of the writings of the Greek philosopher Aristotle [ar′ə stot′l] (384–322 B.C.), whose work on logic, the *Categories*, Abelard mentions, was of primary importance in the development of the most influential medieval philosophic system, scholasticism.

---

There are many seeming contradictions and even obscurities in the innumerable writings of the Church fathers. Our respect for their authority
5 should not stand in the way of an effort on our part to come at the truth. The obscurity and contradictions in ancient writings may be explained upon many grounds, and may be discussed without
10 impugning the good faith and insight of the fathers. . . .

In view of these considerations, I have ventured to bring together various dicta [comments] of the holy fathers, as
15 they came to mind, and to formulate certain questions which were suggested by the seeming contradictions in the statements. These questions ought to serve to excite tender readers to zealous
20 inquiry into truth and so sharpen their wits. The master key of knowledge is indeed, a persistent and frequent questioning. Aristotle, the most clearsighted of all the philosophers, was
25 desirous above all things else to arouse this questioning spirit, for in his *Categories* he exhorts a student as follows: "It may well be difficult to reach a positive conclusion in these matters unless
30 they be frequently discussed. It is by no means fruitless to be doubtful on particular points." By doubting we come to examine, and by examining we reach the truth.

Abelard then presented 158 problems to which he provided the arguments for (yes) and against (no). Here are just a few examples:

---

Should human faith be based upon reason, or no?
Is God the author of evil, or no?
Do we sometimes sin unwillingly, or
5   no?
Does God punish the same sin both here and in the future, or no?
Is it worse to sin openly than secretly, or no?

Contemplating a sphere labeled "philosophy," Pierre Abelard broods in a 19th-century French portrait.

Delivering a sermon to his fellow monks, St. Bernard, abbot of Clairvaux [cler vō′], is shown in this painting by the French artist Jean Fouquet [fü kā′] (c. 1420–c. 1481). St. Bernard dominated religious life in western Europe in the first half of the 12th century.

there is in heaven above and in the earth beneath which he deigns to confess ignorance of: he raises his eyes to
10 heaven and searches the deep things of God and . . . brings back unspeakable words which it is not lawful for a man to utter, while he is . . . prepared to give a reason for everything, even for those
15 things which are above reason; he presumes against reason and against faith. For what is more against reason than by reason to attempt to transcend reason? And what is more against faith than to
20 be unwilling to believe what reason cannot attain? . . .

And so he promises understanding to his hearers, even on those most sublime and sacred truths which are hidden in
25 the very bosom of our holy faith; and he places degrees in the Trinity, modes in the Majesty, numbers in the Eternity. . . . Who does not shudder at such novel profanities of words and
30 ideas?

Needless to say, Abelard soon came under attack by many of the elders of the Church. His most famous and powerful critic was St. Bernard (1090–1153). Bernard devoted his life to setting a pious example to others, ministering to the poor, writing letters of advice to rulers, and defending the Church from the threat of new ideas such as Abelard's. Here is Bernard's attack on Abelard.

We have in France an old teacher turned into a new theologian, who in his early days amused himself with dialectics and who now gives utter-
5 ance to wild imaginations upon the Holy Scriptures. . . . I know not what

## Discussing the Reading

1. According to Abelard, how does one arrive at the truth? Why did St. Bernard find this approach so objectionable?

2. Compare the meaning of lines 18–23 in the first passage from *Sic et Non* to that of lines 17–21 in St. Bernard's attack on Abelard. With which position do you agree?

**CRITICAL THINKING**
**Making Decisions**

In the conduct of your life, do you rely more on faith or on reason? To take an everyday example, when you meet people for the first time, do you tend to rely on your intuition in reacting to them, or do you want to find out something about them on which to base a considered judgment?

# How King John Was Forced to Sign the Magna Carta

**TIME FRAME**

*Early 13th century*

**GEOGRAPHIC SETTING**

*England*

Although the principles expressed in the Magna Carta [mag′nə kär′tə; from Latin, "great charter"] laid the foundation for the rights of people in democratic societies today, King John did not agree to them willingly at all. The following description of the events leading up to the signing of the Magna Carta in 1215 were recorded by a monk who lived through the period. Notice that the barons of England led the struggle against John, but as many scholars have observed, the barons might not have been successful if they had not received support from the merchants of London.

In Easter week of this same year, the above-mentioned nobles assembled at Stamford, with horses and arms; for they had now induced almost all the no-
5 bility of the whole kingdom to join them, and constituted a very large army; for in their army there were computed to be two thousand knights, besides horse soldiers, attendants, and

In the 19th-century mural below, a reluctant King John is pictured at the meadow of Runnymede on June 15, 1215, about to agree to the demands of his barons as expressed in Magna Carta. Four days later the articles were written out, and copies were distributed throughout the kingdom.

foot soldiers, who were variously equipped. . . . and when the king learned this, he sent . . . to them to inquire what the laws and liberties were which they demanded. The barons then delivered to the messengers a paper, containing in great measure the laws and ancient customs of the kingdom, and declared that, unless the king immediately granted them and confirmed them under his own seal, they would, by taking possession of his fortresses, force him to give them sufficient satisfaction as to their before-named demands. . . . The king when he heard the purport of these heads, derisively said, with the greatest indignation, ''Why, amongst these unjust demands, did not the barons ask for my kingdom also? Their demands are vain and visionary, and are unsupported by any plea of reason whatever.'' And at length he angrily declared with an oath, that he would never grant them such liberties as would render him their slave. . . .

There also came to [the barons] there messengers from the city of London, secretly telling them, if they wished to get into that city, to come there immediately. The barons [were] inspired . . . for the rich citizens were favorable to the barons, and the poor ones were afraid to murmur against them. The barons having thus got into the city, placed their own guards in charge of each of the gates, and then arranged all matters in the city at will. They then took [loans] from the citizens. . . .

King John, when he saw that he was deserted by almost all, so that out of his regal superabundance of followers he scarcely retained seven knights, was much alarmed lest the barons would attack his castles and reduce them without difficulty, as they would find no obstacle to their so doing; and he deceitfully pretended to make peace for a time with the aforesaid barons, and . . . told them that, for the sake of peace, and for the exaltation and honor of the kingdom, he would willingly grant them the laws and liberties they required; he also sent word to the barons by these same messengers, to appoint a fitting day and place to meet and carry all these matters into effect. . . . They in their great joy appointed the fifteenth of June for the king to meet them, at a field lying between Staines and Windsor [called Runnymede]. Accordingly, at the time and place pre-agreed on, the king and nobles came to the appointed conference, and when each party had stationed themselves apart from the other, they began a long discussion about terms of peace and the aforesaid liberties. . . . King John, seeing that he was inferior in strength to the barons, without raising any difficulty, granted the underwritten laws and liberties, and confirmed them by his charter [the Magna Carta].

## Discussing the Reading

1. What made it impossible for King John to do anything but sign the Magna Carta? Was this extortion? Why or why not?

2. Can governments exist without "the consent of the governed"? What constitutes that consent? Did King John have it?

**CRITICAL THINKING**
**Making Inferences**

"The barons [were] inspired . . . for the rich citizens were favorable to the barons, and the poor ones were afraid to murmur against them." What inference concerning the attitude of ordinary English people toward the monarchy can you make from this passage? What might account for this attitude?

At the right is a detail of the carved altar-piece of the Royal Chapel of Granada, which commemorates the victories of Ferdinand and Isabella in their war to expel the final Spanish Muslims, or Moors. This detail shows Boabdil [bō' äb-dēl'], the last Moorish king of Granada, leaving the city after turning over the keys to the Spaniards. Behind him, Moorish hostages are pictured filing through the gates of the Alhambra [al-ham'brə], the palace of the Moorish kings of Granada.

# Ferdinand of Aragon— A New Type of King

## 12 B

**TIME FRAME**

*Early 16th century*

**GEOGRAPHIC SETTING**

*Spain*

Between 1000 and 1600 the decentralized government system of feudalism was gradually replaced by what scholars call national monarchies. These were centralized states with a strong king or queen ruling over people who usually shared one language. The unity of these monarchies was sometimes achieved through royal marriages which combined previously separate states. Unity was also achieved by force, through defeat of one group in civil war, or through conquering neighboring states. Ferdinand of Aragon (1452–1516) and Isabella of Castile (1451–1504) used both marriage and conquest to unite Spain. One of their great admirers was the Italian statesman and political philosopher Niccolò Machiavelli [mak'ē ə vel'e] (1469–1527) who

believed that the use of force, not Christian mercy, was the only way to govern successfully. In the following passage from his famous study of the art of ruling, *The Prince*, Machiavelli analyzed the reasons for Ferdinand's success as a king.

Nothing gives a prince more prestige than undertaking great enterprises and setting a splendid example for his people. In our day we have Ferdi-
5 nand of Aragon, the present king of Spain. He may be considered a new prince, since from being a weak king he has risen to become, for fame and glory, the first prince of Christendom; and if
10 you consider his actions, you will find

all of them very great and some of them extraordinary. At the beginning of his reign he attacked Granada [the last Muslim state in Spain], and that enter- prise was the cornerstone of his reign. For some time he carried on the siege in a leisurely way, and without any out- side distractions; he kept all the barons of Castile preoccupied with it, and while they were thinking of the war, they never considered the changes he was making in the state. Thus he acquired reputation and authority over them without their being aware of it. Money from the Church and the people ena- bled him to recruit big armies, and in the course of this long war, to build a military establishment which has since won him much honor. Apart from this,

he made use of the pretext of religion to prepare the way for still greater proj- ects, and adopted a policy of pious cru- elty in expelling the Moors [Muslims] from his kingdom and despoiling them; his conduct here could not have been more despicable nor more unusual. On the same pretext, he attacked [North] Africa; he carried out a campaign in Italy; and finally he assaulted France. Thus he has always been planning and carrying out some great design which has enthralled and preoccupied the minds of his subjects, and kept them fascinated with the outcome of his schemes. And his various projects have risen one out of the other, so that they have never allowed men leisure to take concerted action against him.

The miniature at the right pictures an earlier phase of the *Recon- quista* [rā kon kēs′ tə], or "reconquest" of Spain from the Moors. Ferdinand III (1201?–1252), king of Castile and Leon, is shown receiving the key to the city of Seville, taken by him from the Moors in 1248.

## Discussing the Reading

1. Paraphrase lines 16–24. Evaluate this approach to acquiring and keeping power. What 20th-cen- tury examples can you give to support your evaluation?

2. According to Machiavelli, how did Ferdinand use the "pretext of reli- gion" to increase his prestige? (See lines 29–34.) Was this eth- ical? Machiavelli considered this policy brutal but effective, and called Ferdinand a "splendid example" for his people. What does this estimate indicate about Machiavelli's political theory?

3. Using Machiavelli's explanation of "prestige," who are the most "prestigious" world leaders today? Why?

### CRITICAL THINKING
### Making Hypotheses

Using the experiences of King John (see Reading 12A) and King Ferdinand as your data, create a hypothesis to explain why a ruler keeps or loses power.

# Empress Theodora Speaks Her Mind

**TIME FRAME**
*Early 6th century* A.D.

**GEOGRAPHIC SETTING**
*Constantinople*

Constantinople, the turbulent capital of the Byzantine Empire, was the scene of many popular rebellions during its long history. The most famous of these was the Nika [nī′kə] Revolt, which occurred in 532, early in the reign of the greatest Byzantine emperor, Justinian [ju stin′ē ən], who ruled from 527 to 565. The revolt began when the Blues and the Greens, the two factions who competed in the chariot races at Constantinople's huge arena, the Hippodrome, united in opposition to the expense of the wars waged by Justinian to expand his empire. For seven days the rioters surged through the streets of Constantinople, shouting their cry of *Nika* (the Greek word meaning "victory") as they burned and looted. Wealthy people fled the city. Justinian, his wife Theodora [thē ə dô′ rə] (?–548), and various government officials shut themselves up in the imperial palace. One eyewitness was the historian Procopius [prō cō′ pē əs] (490?–562?), who was an adviser to Justinian's general, Belisarius [bel i sā′ rē əs]. (It was Belisarius who eventually suppressed the rebellion, killing thirty thousand of the rioters in the process.) In the following passage, Procopius described how the Emperor was persuaded not to flee his capital.

**M**eanwhile, all of the citizens who were sane-minded were fleeing to the opposite mainland, and fire was applied to the city as if it had fallen
5 under the hand of an enemy. The sanctuary of Sophia [sō fē′ə] and the baths of Zeuxippus [züks ip′pəs], and the portion of the imperial residence from the propylaea [prop′ə lē′ə; a vestibule
10 or antichamber] as far as the so-called House of Ares [er′ēz] were destroyed by fire, and besides these both the great colonnades which extended as far as the

In the twenty-one years of her reign, Theodora's sound political instincts saved the throne for her husband Justinian several times. Theodora is shown at the left, in a detail from a 6th-century mosaic in the church of San Vitale at Ravenna. At the right is another mosaic from San Vitale, showing Justinian and his advisers celebrating the consecration of the church.

marketplace which bears the name of Constantine, in addition to many houses of wealthy men and a vast amount of treasure. During this time the emperor and his [wife] with a few members of the senate shut themselves up in the palace and remained quietly there. . . .

Now the emperor and his court were deliberating as to whether it would be better for them if they remained or if they took to flight in the ships. And many opinions were expressed favoring either course. And the Empress Theodora also spoke to the following effect: "As to the belief that a woman ought not to be daring among men or to assert herself boldly among those who are holding back from fear, I consider that the present crisis most certainly does not permit us to discuss whether the matter should be regarded in this or in some other way. For in the case of those whose interests have come into the greatest danger nothing else seems best except to settle the issue immediately before them in the best possible way. My opinion then is that the present time, above all others, is inopportune for flight, even though it bring safety. For while it is impossible for a man who has seen the light not also to die, for one who has been an emperor it is unendurable to be a fugitive. May I never be separated from this purple [a color only royalty could wear], and may I not live that day on which those who meet me shall not address me as mistress. If, now, it is your wish to save yourself, O Emperor, there is no difficulty. For we have much money, and there is the sea, here the boats. However consider whether it will not come about after you have been saved that you would gladly exchange that safety for death. For as for myself, I approve a certain ancient saying that royalty is a good burial-shroud." When the queen had spoken thus, all were filled with boldness, and, turning their thoughts towards resistance, they began to consider how they might be able to defend themselves if any hostile force should come against them.

## Discussing the Reading

1. What was Theodora's advice and how valuable was it? What were the results of her words?

2. Explain the meaning of the saying quoted by Theodora, "Royalty is a good burial-shroud."

### CRITICAL THINKING
### Making Generalizations

This reading indicates one of the few ways women could acquire political power. Why was Theodora so powerful? Was she an exceptional woman? Was she an exceptional leader?

# The Revenge of Olga, Princess of Kiev

13B

**TIME FRAME**
*Mid-10th century* A.D.

**GEOGRAPHIC SETTING**
*Russia*

The first Russian state was formed by Prince Oleg in 882, with the city of Kiev [kē′ef] at its center. He was a powerful and successful ruler, but his son Igor who ruled after him was harsh and greedy. He was killed in 945 by a Slavic people called the Derevlians [də rev′lē ənz] from whom he tried to collect triple the amount of tribute they owed. The Derevlians then went to Kiev to force Igor's widow Olga to marry their prince. The following account from the *Primary Chronicle* of Russian history, kept by Russian monks, tells of Olga's revenge upon the Derevlians.

O lga was informed that the Derevlians had arrived, and summoned them to her presence with a gracious welcome. . . . The Derevlians then an-
5 nounced that their tribe had sent them to report that they had slain her husband, because he was like a wolf, crafty and ravening, but that their princes, who had thus preserved the land of Der-
10 eva, were good, and that Olga should come and marry their Prince Mal. For

the name of the Prince of Dereva was Mal.

Olga made this reply: "Your proposal
15 is pleasing to me; indeed, my husband cannot rise again from the dead. But I desire to honor you tomorrow in the presence of my people. Return now to your boat, and remain there with an
20 aspect of arrogance. I shall send for you on the morrow, and you shall say, 'We will not ride on horses nor go on foot; carry us [on your shoulders] in our boat.' And you shall be carried in your
25 boat." Thus, she dismissed them to their vessel.

Now Olga gave command that a large deep ditch should be dug in the castle. . . . Thus on the morrow, Olga as
30 she sat in the hall sent for the strangers, and her messengers approached them and said, "Olga summons you to great honor." But they replied, "We will not ride on horseback nor in wagons, nor go
35 on foot; carry us in our boat." The people of Kiev then lamented: "Slavery is our lot. Our prince is killed, and our

princess intends to marry their prince."
So they carried the Derevlians in their
40 boat. The latter sat on the cross-benches
in great robes, puffed up with pride.
They thus were borne into the court
before Olga, and when the men had
brought the Derevlians in, they dropped
45 them into the trench along with the
boat. Olga bent over and inquired
whether they found the honor to their
taste. They answered that it was worse
than the death of Igor. She then com-
50 manded that they should be buried
alive, and they were thus buried. . . .

Olga then sent to the Derevlians the
following message: "I am now coming
to you, so prepare great quantities of
55 mead in the city where you killed my
husband, that I may weep over his grave
and hold a funeral feast for him." When
they heard these words, they gathered
great quantities of honey, and brewed
60 mead. Taking a small escort, Olga made
the journey with ease, and upon her
arrival at Igor's tomb, she wept for her
husband. She bade her followers pile up
a great mound, and when they had piled
65 it up, she also gave command that a
funeral feast should be held. Thereupon
the Derevlians sat down to drink, and
Olga bade her followers wait upon
them.
70 The Derevlians inquired of Olga

where the retinue was which they had
sent to meet her. She replied that they
were following with her husband's
bodyguard. When the Derevlians were
75 drunk, she bade her followers fall upon
them, and went about herself egging on
her retinue to the Massacre of the Derevlians. So they cut down five thousand
of them; but Olga returned to Kiev and
80 prepared an army to attack the survi-
vors.

As Olga watches, a group of Derevlians is burned alive in the illustration from an old Russian chronicle on the facing page. The manuscript illustration above shows Olga ordering the burial of the first Derevlian envoys, boat and all, while they are still alive.

## Discussing the Reading

1. What is the lesson of this story? How valuable is this lesson in politics today?

2. Why did the Derevlians insist that Olga marry their Prince Mal? Review the introduction to Reading 12B. Why did Ferdinand and Isabella marry? Review Reading 10B. Why did Charlemagne object to the marriage of his daughters? From these three readings, what can you generalize about the nature of royal marriages? What was the value of a daughter to a royal family?

**CRITICAL THINKING**
**Synthesizing Information**

How would Machiavelli rate Olga as a leader? Defend your answer.

# In the Name of Allah

# 14A

**TIME FRAME**
*Early 7th century* A.D.

**GEOGRAPHIC SETTING**
*Arabia*

Muslims believe the *Koran* contains the very words of Allah [al′ə], or God; and, except for a few passages in which Muhammad speaks, the speaker throughout is Allah. The *Koran* is also a masterpiece of Arabic literature, and most people who read Arabic feel that no translation can do justice to the rhythm and balance of the original. However, the following selection from one *surah*

[sûr′ə], or chapter, does give some idea of the moral message of the *Koran* and the continuity with Judaism and Christianity that Islam maintains.

We [God] first created man from an essence of clay: then placed him, a living germ, in a safe enclosure.

Below on the left is the key that once locked the Great Mosque at Mecca, which surrounds the Kaaba [kä'-bə], Islam's most sacred shrine. Below on the right is a page from a 14th- or 15th-century manuscript of the *Koran*.

The germ We made a clot of blood, and the clot a lump of flesh. This We fashioned into bones, then clothed the bones with flesh, thus bringing forth another creation. Blessed be Allah, the noblest of creators! . . .

We sent forth Noah to his people. "Serve Allah, my people," he said, "for you have no god but Him. Will you not take heed?"

The unbelieving elders of his people said: "This man is but a mortal like you, feigning himself your superior. Had Allah willed, He could have sent down angels. Nor did such a thing happen to our forefathers. He is surely possessed. Keep an eye on him awhile."

Noah said: "Help, me Lord. They will not believe me."

We revealed Our will to him, saying: "Build an ark under Our watchful eye, according to Our instructions. When Our judgment comes to pass and water wells out from the oven, take aboard a

54

pair from every species and the members of your household, except those of them already doomed. Do not plead with Me for those who have done wrong: they shall be drowned. And when you and all your followers have gone aboard, say 'Praise be to Allah who has delivered us from a sinful nation. Lord, let my landing from this ark be blessed. You alone can make me land in safety.' " . . .

Then We sent Moses and his brother Aaron with Our signs and with clear authority to Pharaoh and his nobles. But they received them with scorn, for they were arrogant men. "What!" they said. "Are we to believe in two mortals like yourselves, whose people are our bondsmen [slaves]?" They denied them, and thus incurred destruction. And We gave Moses the Torah [tôr'ə; the Jewish law], so that his people might be rightly guided.

We made the son of Mary [Jesus] and his mother a sign to mankind and gave them a shelter on a peaceful hillside watered by a fresh spring.

Apostles! Eat of that which is wholesome and do good works: I have knowledge of all your actions. Your religion is but one religion, and I am your only Lord: therefore fear Me.

Yet men have divided themselves into different sects, each rejoicing in its own doctrines. Leave them in their error till death overtakes them.

Do they think that in giving them wealth and children We are solicitous for their welfare? By no means! They cannot see.

Those who walk in fear of their Lord; who believe in the revelations of their Lord; who worship none besides their Lord; who give alms with their hearts filled with awe, knowing that they will return to their Lord: these vie with each other for salvation and are the first to attain it.

## Discussing the Reading

1. Is Islam an eastern or a western religion? Why?

2. As indicated by this surah of the *Koran,* what stories are part of the tradition of Judaism, Christianity, and Islam?

### CRITICAL THINKING
### Assessing Cause and Effect

As this reading makes clear, Judaism, Christianity, and Islam have much in common. What causes the prejudice, conflicts, and persecutions that have marked the contacts of these beliefs with one another?

# The Battle of Hattin

# 14B

**TIME FRAME**
*Late 12th century*

**GEOGRAPHIC SETTING**
*Palestine*

After their conquest of Jerusalem in 1099, the French princes and nobles of the First Crusade established a number of small states in Syria and Palestine. During the next two centuries, Islam began to rally against these invaders, and one by one the Crusader States fell. The most famous Islamic leader in the reconquest of the Near East was Saladin [sal'ə dən] (1137?–1193), the sultan of Egypt and Syria. Saladin became legendary even among his Christian opponents for his chivalrous conduct of war. A gifted statesman as well as a brilliant soldier, he preferred negotiation to battle. "Abstain from the shedding of blood," he once said; "Trust not to that; for blood that is spilt never slumbers." To keep the Muslims united, Saladin proclaimed a *jihad* [ji häd'], or holy war, against the

Christians. He attacked the Crusader States and recaptured Jerusalem. The decisive battle in this campaign was fought near the village of Hattin in northern Palestine on July 4, 1187. The following account of Saladin's great victory is by the Islamic historian Ibn al-Athir [ib'ən äl ä'thər]. (He refers to the Crusaders as "Franks," the usual term employed by Muslims to describe their Christian opponents, many of whom came from France.)

W hen the Franks learned that Saladin had attacked Tiberias [tī-bir'ē əs; a city in nothern Palestine] and taken it and everything in it, burn-
5 ing the houses and anything they could not remove, they met to take counsel. . . . The generals decided to advance and give battle to the Muslims, so they left the place where they had been en-
10 camped until now and advanced on the Muslim army. When Saladin received the news he ordered his army to withdraw from its position near Tiberias; his only reason for besieging Tiberias was
15 to make the Franks abandon their position and offer battle. The Muslims went down to the water [of the Sea of Galilee]. The weather was blazingly hot and the Franks, who were suffering greatly
20 from thirst, were prevented by the Muslims from reaching the water. They had drained all the local cisterns, but could not turn back for fear of the Muslims. So they passed that night tormented with
25 thirst. The Muslims for their part had lost their first fear of the enemy and were in high spirits, and spent the night inciting one another to battle. They could smell victory in the air, and the
30 more they saw of the unexpectedly low morale of the Franks the more aggressive and daring they became; throughout the night the cries *Allah akbar* ["God is great"] and "there is no God

35 but Allah" rose up to heaven. Meanwhile the Sultan was deploying the vanguard of archers and distributing the arrows.

On Saturday 4 July 1187 Saladin and
40 the Muslims mounted their horses and advanced on the Franks. They too were mounted, and the two armies came to blows. The Franks were suffering badly from thirst, and had lost confidence.
45 The battle raged furiously, both sides putting up a tenacious resistance. The Muslim archers sent up clouds of arrows like thick swarms of locusts, killing many of the Frankish horses. The
50 Franks, surrounding themselves with their infantry, tried to fight their way toward Tiberias in the hope of reaching water, but Saladin realized their objective and forestalled them by planting
55 himself and his army in the way. He himself rode up and down the Muslim lines encouraging and restraining his troops where necessary. The whole army obeyed his commands and re-
60 spected his prohibitions. One of his young mamluks [mam'lūks; slaves serving as soldiers] led a terrifying charge on the Franks and performed prodigious feats of valor until he was
65 overwhelmed by numbers and killed, when all the Muslims charged the enemy lines and almost broke through, slaying many Franks in the process. The Count [of Tripoli, ruler of one of the
70 Crusader States] saw that the situation was desperate and realized that he could not withstand the Muslim army, so by agreement with his companions he charged the lines before him. The
75 commander of that section of the Muslim army was Taqi ad-Din 'Umar [tä'kē äd dēn' ü'mär], Saladin's nephew. When he saw that the Franks charging his lines were desperate and
80 that they were going to try to break through, he sent orders for a passage to be made for them through the ranks.

One of the volunteers had set fire to the dry grass that covered the ground; it took fire and the wind carried the heat and smoke down on the enemy. They had to endure thirst, the summer's heat, the blazing fire and smoke and the fury of battle. When the Count fled the Franks lost heart and were on the verge of surrender, but seeing that the only way to save their lives was to defy death, they made a series of charges that almost dislodged the Muslims from their position in spite of their numbers, had not the grace of God been with them. As each wave of attackers fell back they left their dead behind them; their numbers diminished rapidly, while the Muslims were all around them like a circle about its diameter. The surviving Franks made for a hill near Hattin, where they hoped to pitch their tents and defend themselves. They were vigorously attacked from all sides and prevented from pitching more than one tent, that of the King. The Muslims captured their great cross, called the "True Cross," in which they say is a piece of wood upon which, according to them, the Messiah was crucified. This was one of the heaviest blows that could be inflicted on them and made their death and destruction certain. Large numbers of their cavalry and infantry were killed or captured. The King stayed on the hillside with five hundred of the most gallant and famous knights.

I was told that al-Malik al-Afdal [äl mäl'ēk äl äf'däl], Saladin's son, said: "I was at my father Saladin's side during that battle, the first that I saw with my own eyes. The Frankish King had retreated to the hill with his band,

Saladin seizes the relic of the True Cross from his Christian foes at the Battle of Hattin in this illustration from a 13th-century French manuscript.

and from there he led a furious charge against the Muslims facing him, forcing them back upon my father. I saw that he was alarmed and distraught, and he tugged at his beard as he went forward crying: 'Away with the Devil's lie!' The Muslims turned to counterattack and drove the Franks back up the hill. When I saw the Franks retreating before the Muslim onslaught I cried out for joy: 'We have conquered them!' But they returned to the charge with undiminished ardor and drove our army back toward my father. His response was the same as before, and the Muslims counterattacked and drove the Franks back to the hill. Again I cried: 'We have beaten them!' but my father turned to me and said: 'Be quiet; we shall not have beaten them until that tent falls!' As he spoke the tent fell, and the Sultan dismounted and prostrated himself in the thanks of God, weeping for joy." This was how the tent fell: the Franks had been suffering terribly from thirst during that charge, which they hoped would win them a way out of their distress, but the way of escape was blocked. They dismounted and sat down on the ground and the Muslims fell upon them, pulled down the King's tent and captured every one of them, including the King [of Jerusalem, ruler of one of the Crusader States]. . . . The number of dead and captured was so large that those who saw the slain could not believe that anyone could have been taken alive, and those who saw the prisoners could not believe that any had been killed. From the time of their first assault on Palestine in 1098 until now the Franks had never suffered such a defeat.

---

## Discussing the Reading

1. Review the reasons that the Christians had been successful in the First Crusade. (See Reading 11A.) In 1187 what advantages did the Muslims have?

2. What was Saladin's strategy? What tactics did he use to achieve this strategy? Explain the difference between strategy and tactics.

3. What role did geography play in the battle?

### CRITICAL THINKING
### Evaluating Sources of Information

On a scale of 1 to 5 (with 5 the highest), rate the objectivity of this account of the battle. Review Reading 11A. Rate the objectivity of that account. Defend your ratings. In an evaluation of historical writing, what else should be considered besides objectivity?

---

# The Desert and the City

15A

**TIME FRAME**
*Late 7th century;*
*12th century*

**GEOGRAPHIC SETTING**
*Middle East*

The Muslim world had a single religion but many different styles of life and cultures. The two poems in this reading not only illustrate this diversity, but they also show how deeply attached people were to the way of life they knew best.

The first Umayyad [ü mī'yad] ruler, or caliph [kā'lif], Mu'awiya [mü ä'wē ə], was surrounded by many Arab soldiers and family who still had ties to the nomadic desert life. His wife, Maisuna [mī sü'nə], was a Bedouin (nomadic) Arab and an accomplished poet. She married Mu'awiya at an early age, and as he became more successful, building mosques and palaces in Damascus,

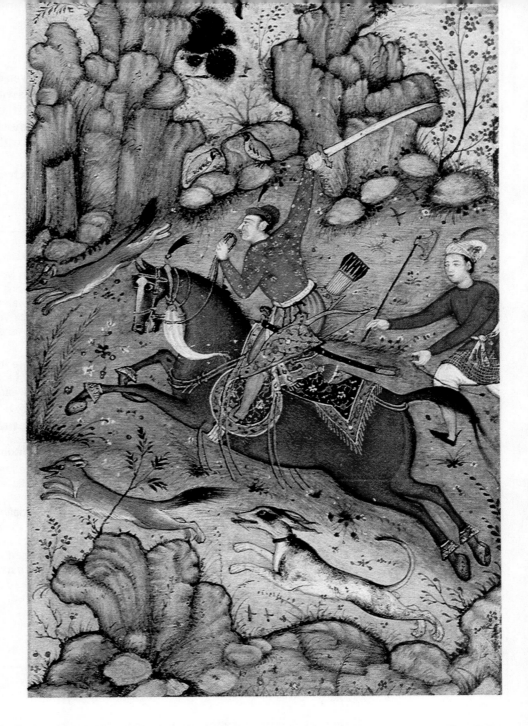

A prince hunts with his hounds in this illustration from a *Divan* [di-van'; Persian meaning "works"] of Anwari that dates from the 16th century.

Jerusalem, and other great cities, she became more and more homesick for her old desert way of life. One day her husband overheard her singing the following poem that she had composed, and he became so angry with her that he banished her and her son from his palace and sent them back to the desert.

The coarse cloth worn in the
   serenity of the desert
Is more precious to me than the
   luxurious robes of a queen;
5 I love the Bedouin's tent, caressed by
   the murmuring breeze, and standing

amid boundless horizons,
More than the gilded halls of marble in
all their royal splendor.
10 I feel more at ease with my simple crust,
Than with the delicacies of the court;
I prefer to rise early with the caravan,
Rather than be in the golden glare of the
sumptuous escort.
15 The barking of a watchdog keeping
away strangers
Pleases me more than the sounds of the
tambourine played by the court
singers;
20 I prefer a desert cavalier, generous and
poor,
To a fat lout in purple living behind
closed doors.

Following is a portion of a poem written in the 12th century by Anwari [än wä′rē], a poet from Baghdad. Notice how, in contrast to Maisuna's poem, Anwari praised the city and viewed it as a desirable place to live.

H ail to Baghdad, home of culture
and art,
The unique city of this world!
Its suburbs are colorful embroideries
5 And its breeze is the breath of life.
Each of its stones is an agate, showering
pearls,
And its earth a fragrant amber.
The Turkish beauties, with bodies like
silver,
10

Made a heaven on the banks of Tigris,
And the girls with ravishing faces like
the rays of the moon
Built a paradise in the heart of Rahba.
15 Tigris itself, with the thousand glittering
boats,
Appears as a heaven in its starry
splendor.

## Discussing the Reading

1. Compare Maisuna's and Anwari's descriptions of city life. What similarities are there in the two accounts? What can you conclude is an accurate depiction of the city?

2. What were the attractions of desert life for Maisuna? What were the attractions of city life? Which do you prefer? Why?

**CRITICAL THINKING**
**Evaluating Sources of Information**

Compare Maisuna's life with that of the blacksmith's wife in Reading 9A. How does each woman define her own sense of worth in relation to her husband? Are their views of each society objective? Explain. How could you get a more objective view? Is prose more objective than poetry?

# How al-Razi Cured the Amir

15B

**TIME FRAME**
*Late 9th-early 10th century*

**GEOGRAPHIC SETTING**
*Afghanistan*

Al-Razi [äl rä′zē] (852?–932?) was probably the greatest of all Muslim physicians. His careful observations and descriptions of disease symptoms and fever patterns are still fine examples of scientific medical studies today. In the following account, however, al-Razi demonstrated that sometimes healing requires mental as well as physical treatment. The story

concerns an amir [ə mir′], or king, of Afghanistan who was so ill (with what we do not know) that he could not stand. Al-Razi's initial treatments did not cure him.

O ne day he [al-Razi] came in before
the Amir and said, "Tomorrow I
am going to try another method of treat-

فاذا اردالعصير فصفه فهذا الشراب موافق لوجع الحلق والجنب وال
والاسهال والارتفاع ولمن به لغم غليظ فى حلقه يصفى اللون وكثر النو

وليس له غائلة موافق للمثانه والكلا

م م م م م م

Above is a page from a 13th-century Islamic medical manuscript, giving a recipe for cough medicine and picturing the doctor's preparation of it.

hand], came in, and stood for a while reviling the Amir, saying, "O such-and-such, . . . If I do not destroy thee as a 30 punishment for this, I am no true son of [my father]!"

The Amir was furious and rose from his place to his knees. Al-Razi drew a knife and threatened him yet more, 35 until the Amir, partly from anger, partly from fear, completely rose to his feet. When al-Razi saw the Amir on his feet, he turned around and went out from the bath, and both he and his servant 40 mounted, the one the horse, the other the mule, and turned their faces towards the Oxus [ok′səs; a river that forms part of the northern border of Afghanistan]. At the time of the after- 45 noon prayer they crossed the river, and halted nowhere till they reached Merv [a distant town]. When al-Razi alighted at Merv, he wrote a letter to the Amir, saying, "May the life of the Amir be pro- 50 longed in health of body and effective command! I your servant undertook the treatment and did all that was possible. There was, however, an extreme failure in the [body's heat], and the treatment 55 of the disease by ordinary means would have been a protracted affair. I therefore abandoned it in favor of [emotional] treatment, carried you to the hot bath, administered a draught, and left you so 60 long as to bring about a [partial treat-ment of the disease-causing fluids]. Then I angered the Amir, so as to aid the [body's heat], and it gained strength until those [fluids], already [partially 65 treated], were dissolved. But henceforth it is not expedient that a meeting should take place between myself and the Amir."

Now after the Amir had risen to his 70 feet and al-Razi had gone out and ridden off, the Amir at once fainted. When he came to himself he went forth from the bath and called to his servants, saying, "Where has the physician gone?" They

ment, but for the carrying out of it you 5 will have to sacrifice such-and-such a horse and such-and-such a mule," the two being animals noted for their speed, so that in one night they would go [over 150 miles].

10 So next day he took the Amir to the hot bath . . . outside the palace, leaving that horse and mule ready equipped and tightly girt in the charge of his own servant at the door of the bath; while of 15 the Amir's retinue and attendants he suffered not one to enter the bath. Then he brought the Amir into the middle chamber of the hot bath, and poured over him tepid water, after which he 20 prepared a draught, tasted it, and gave it to him to drink. And he kept him there till such time as the [disease-causing fluids] in his joints had [been partially treated].

25 Then he himself went out and put on his clothes, and [taking a knife in his

answered, "He came out from the bath, and mounted the horse, while his attendant mounted the mule, and went off."

Then the Amir knew what object he had had in view. So he came forth on his own feet from the hot bath; and tidings of this ran through the city. Then he gave audience, and his servants and retainers and people rejoiced greatly, and gave alms, and offered sacrifices, and held high festival.

<sub>75</sub> — <sub>80</sub> — <sub>85</sub>

---

## Discussing the Reading

1. Describe al-Razi's cure. What does this story suggest about human nature?

2. Do you think al-Razi's method was appropriate? Would a similar approach ever be appropriate for a doctor today? What circumstances might require such an approach?

**CRITICAL THINKING**
**Identifying Assumptions**

In order for al-Razi to choose the method of treatment that he used to cure the Amir, he needed to rely on certain assumptions about the nature of his patient's illness and personality. What were these assumptions?

---

# Chinese Paper Money

16A

**TIME FRAME**
*Late 12th century*

**GEOGRAPHIC SETTING**
*China*

One of the things that most astonished the Italian traveler Marco Polo (1254?–1324?) during his visit to China in the late 13th century was the use of paper money. Today we take paper money for granted, but to Europeans of Polo's time only gold or silver had real value. In the following excerpt from his *Travels*, Marco Polo described how Chinese money was kept valuable by the decree of the Chinese emperor, Kublai Khan [kü′blī kän′] (1216?–1294), and the emperor's ability to redeem the paper currency with government wealth.

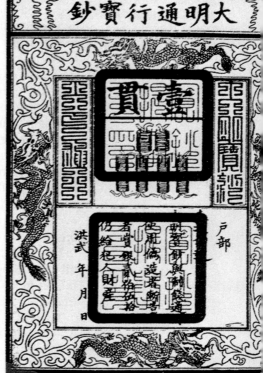

At the right is a piece of 14th-century Chinese currency. Although this bill was printed perhaps a hundred years after the visit of Marco Polo, it is similar to the paper money he described in his *Travels*.

Now that I have told you in detail of the splendor of this city of the Emperor's, I shall proceed to tell you of the Mint which he hath in the same city, in the which he hath his money coined and struck, as I shall relate to you. . . .

He makes [the workers at the mint]

<sub>5</sub>

The Polos embark for China from Venice in the scene at right, taken from a 14th-century manuscript. Marco Polo, with his father and his uncle, set out in 1271. He did not return home until twenty-four years later.

take of the bark of a certain tree, in fact of the mulberry tree, the leaves of which
10 are the food of the silkworms—these trees being so numerous that whole districts are full of them. What they take is a certain fine white bast or skin which lies between the wood of the tree and
15 the thick outer bark, and this they make into something resembling sheets of paper, but black. When these sheets have been prepared they are cut up into pieces of different sizes. The smallest of
20 these sizes is worth a half tornese [tôr nā′zā; a small silver or copper coin]; the next, a little larger, one tornese ; one, a little larger still, is worth half a silver groat [grōt; a more valuable
25 coin] of Venice; another a whole groat; . . . All these pieces of paper are issued with as much solemnity and authority as if they were of pure gold or silver; and on every piece a variety of
30 officials, whose duty it is, have to write their names, and to put their seals. And when all is prepared duly, the chief officer deputed by the Khan smears the seal entrusted to him with vermilion
35 [vər mil′yən; a bright red pigment], and impresses it on the paper, so that the

form of the seal remains printed upon it in red; the money is then authentic. Any one forging it would be punished with
40 death. And the Khan causes every year to be made such a vast quantity of this money, which costs him nothing, that it must equal in amount all the treasure in the world.
45 With these pieces of paper, made as I have described, he causes all payments on his own account to be made; and he makes them to pass current universally
50 over all his kingdoms and provinces and territories, and whithersoever his power and sovereignty extends. And nobody, however important he may think himself, dares to refuse them on
55 pain of death. And indeed everybody takes them readily, for wheresoever a person may go throughout the Great Khan's dominions he shall find these pieces of paper current, and shall be
60 able to transact all sales and purchases of goods by means of them just as well as if they were coins of pure gold. And all the while they are so light that ten bezants' [bez′ənts; a bezant was a gold
65 coin] worth does not weigh one golden bezant.

# The Southern Emperor Rules the Southern Land

# 16B

**TIME FRAME**
*11th-15th century*

**GEOGRAPHIC SETTING**
*Vietnam*

China controlled Vietnam from around 100 B.C. to A.D. 900. Then from 939 to the 17th century, while remaining politically independent, Vietnam still had to fight off many invading armies from China. Throughout these centuries Vietnam's culture was strongly influenced by the Chinese, as the following Vietnamese poetry, much of which was written originally in Chinese, demonstrates. In the first poem, Chinese cultural influence on Vietnam is admitted. The "Northerner" of the title is a person from China. Annam [ə nam'], meaning "the Quiet (or Pacified) South," was the name given to Vietnam in the 7th century by its Chinese overlords. The Han and Tang are dynasties of Chinese rulers.

### Reply to a Northerner Who Asked About Annam's Customs

Y ou asked about things of Annam.
   The Quiet South boasts polished ways.
Our king and subjects heed Han laws.
5 Our caps and gowns obey Tang rules.
Jade bottles brim with fresh-brewed wine.

Gold knives carve up delicious fish.
Each year, for two or three full months,
10 spring gardens burst with peach and plum.

In A.D. 39, two famous sisters, Trung Trac [trung träk] and Trung Nhi [trung nē], led a Vietnamese rebellion against the Chinese governor Su Ting. The following poem celebrates their bravery, for in the end their revolt failed and they chose suicide over capture. Lingnan [ling nän'], meaning "south of the mountain range," was the Chinese name for a region that included North Vietnam.

### Homage to the Trung Queens

T o slay the people's foe and wreak revenge,
Two sisters lifted arms for their just cause.
5 One battle put Su Ting's scared wits to rout.
A hundred tribes rose up to guard Lingnan.
Large bounties they bestowed,
10 mounting the throne.

64

Sweet blessings they conferred,
    donning their crowns.
While streams and hills endure, their
    shrine shall stand:
15 A monument to peerless womanhood.

According to tradition, the following poem was written in 1076 and read to troops to encourage them to fight one of many invading Chinese armies.

### The Southern Emperor Rules the Southern Land

The Southern emperor rules the
    Southern land.
Our destiny is writ in Heaven's Book.
How dare you bandits trespass on our
5    soil?
You shall meet your undoing at our
    hands.

Throughout the centuries of struggle the Vietnamese came to rely on their own sense of patriotism and "people's

Below is a painted wooden plate from Vietnam showing the symbol of the yin-yang in the center, surrounded by the eight trigrams used in the ancient Chinese classic of divination, the *I Ching*. The symbols of yin and yang represent the opposed, but interacting forces that create the universe and everything in it.

strength," as much as on military tactics such as blocking rivers to the invaders' boats with stakes and chains, as mentioned in the following poem.

### Blocking the River's Mouth

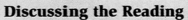

Wood stakes in rows on rows stem
    not the tide.
Sunk iron chains yet fail to shackle
    waves.
5 The people's strength, like water, tips
    the boat.
No rugged terrain frustrates Heaven's
    will.
Evil or good springs not in just one day.
10 A hero's grievance lasts a thousand
    years.
The cosmos holds a sense that never
    ends:
It lurks in this blue stream, those trees,
15    those mists.

## Discussing the Reading

1. What characteristics of the Vietnamese people can you infer from these poems?

2. Would you expect the Chinese and the Vietnamese to be close allies today? Explain.

**CRITICAL THINKING**
**Making Generalizations**

In the 1960s and early 1970s, the United States intervened in a long and destructive civil war between communists and anti-communists in Vietnam. In the end the American-backed anti-communists were defeated. Might it have been useful for American officials to have read patriotic poems like "Homage to the Trung Queens," "The Southern Emperor Rules the Southern Land," and "Blocking the River's Mouth"? What do these poems indicate about the Vietnamese? Justify your answer.

# The Death of Atsumori

**TIME FRAME**
*Late 12th century*
**GEOGRAPHIC SETTING**
*Japan*

By the middle of the 12th century, the Japanese emperor had authority in name only. In 1156 a vicious civil war broke out between two powerful landowning clans, the Taira [tä ē′rä] and the Minamoto [mē nä mō′tō], which finally ended in 1185 with the annihilation of the Taira in a great sea battle. As one literary historian observes, "Stories of the splendors and fall of the Taira, and of the acts of heroism and pathos which marked the wars, were soon being recited by ballad-singers. These stories were assembled, more or less in the present form, by the middle of

Above left is a samurai commander dressed for battle. In his right hand he carries a fan, used to signal his subordinates, encouraging them and giving them directions. Above right is a suit of samurai armor from the Muromachi period (1333–1600).

the 13th century." This cycle of ballads is known as *The Tale of the Heike*. The name *Heike* [hä′kä] refers to the Taira clan. The following episode comes from the latter part of the cycle.

When the Heike were routed at Ichi no tani [ē′chē nō tä′nē], and their nobles and courtiers were fleeing to the shore to escape in their 5 ships, Kumagai Naozane [kü mä′gä ē nä ō zä′nē] came riding along a narrow path onto the beach, with the intention of intercepting one of their great captains. Just then his eye fell on a single 10 horseman who was attempting to reach one of the ships in the offing. The horse he rode was dappled-gray, and its saddle glittered with gold mounting. Not doubting that he was one of the chief 15 captains, Kumagai beckoned to him with his war fan, crying out: "Shameful! to show an enemy your back. Return! Return!"

The warrior turned his horse and 20 rode back to the beach, where Kumagai at once engaged him in mortal combat. Quickly hurling him to the ground, he sprang upon him and tore off his helmet

to cut off his head, when he beheld the 25 face of a youth of sixteen or seventeen, delicately powdered and with blackened teeth, just about the age of his own son and with features of great beauty. "Who are you?" he asked. "Tell me 30 your name, for I would spare your life."

"Nay, first say who you are," replied the young man.

"I am Kumagai Naozane of Musashi [mü sä′shē], a person of no particular 35 importance."

"Then you have made a good capture," said the youth. "Take my head and show it to some of my side, and they will tell you who I am."

40 "Though he is one of their leaders," mused Kumagai, "if I slay him it will not turn victory into defeat, and if I spare him, it will not turn defeat into victory. When my son Kojirō [kō jē′rō] was but 45 slightly wounded at Ichi no tani this morning, did it not pain me? How this young man's father would grieve to hear that he had been killed! I will spare him."

50 Just then, looking behind him, he saw Doi [dō′ē] and Kajiwara [kä jē wä′rä] coming up with fifty horsemen. "Alas! look there," he exclaimed, the tears running down his face, "though I would 55 spare your life, the whole countryside swarms with our men, and you cannot escape them. If you must die, let it be by my hand, and I will see that prayers are said for your rebirth in Paradise."

60 "Indeed it must be so," said the young warrior. "Cut off my head at once."

Kumagai was so overcome by compassion that he could scarcely wield his 65 blade. His eyes swam and he hardly knew what he did, but there was no help for it; weeping bitterly he cut off the boy's head. "Alas!" he cried, "what life is so hard as that of a soldier? Only 70 because I was born of a warrior family must I suffer this affliction! How

lamentable it is to do such cruel deeds!" He pressed his face to the sleeve of his armor and wept bitterly. Then, wrap-
75 ping up the head, he was stripping off the young man's armor when he discovered a flute in a brocade bag. "Ah," he exclaimed, "it was this youth and his friends who were amusing themselves
80 with music within the walls this morning. Among all our men of the Eastern Provinces I doubt if there is any one of them who has brought a flute with him. How gentle the ways of these
85 courtiers!"

When he brought the flute to the Commander, all who saw it were moved to tears; he discovered then that the youth was Atsumori [ät sü mō′rē], the
90 youngest son of Tsunemori [sü-ne mō′rē], aged sixteen years. From this time the mind of Kumagai was turned toward the religious life.

### Discussing the Reading

1. Kumagai says that it would be better for him to be the one that kills Atsumori and the young man agrees. Why might they both feel this way?

2. Why does this experience turn Kumagai toward the religious life? Do you think he will remain a warrior? Why or why not?

**CRITICAL THINKING**
**Synthesizing Information**

What reassurance might Krishna (see Reading 7A) offer Kumagai about the necessity of taking Atsumori's life?

# The Japanese Tea Ceremony

# 17B

**TIME FRAME**
*16th century-present*

**GEOGRAPHIC SETTING**
*Japan*

In 1191 a Zen Buddhist monk introduced Japan to the Chinese practice of tea drinking. In the 16th century the Japanese tea ceremony became a highly refined activity, yet one in which almost every family engaged. It was meant to be a meditative activity, when the cares of the world were forgotten. All was to be perfectly clean; the tea sipped, not gulped. An object of beauty or nature was the sole focus of attention. In wealthy homes special teahouses were constructed, set in peaceful gardens (as described in the reading below). The tea ceremony is still common in Japan today, and its ritual remains essentially unchanged. The following description was written in the late 19th century by a famous Japanese art critic, Okakura Kakuzo [o kä′kü rä kä kü′zō] (1862–1913), and includes a story about the first and greatest Japanese "tea master," Rikiu [rē kē′ü] (1521–1591).

The average Westerner, in his sleek complacency, will see in the tea ceremony but another instance of the thousand and one oddities which con-
5 stitute the quaintness and childishness of the East to him. He was [accustomed] to regard Japan as barbarous while she indulged in the gentle arts of peace: he calls her civilized since she began to
10 commit wholesale slaughter on [Chinese] battlefields. Much comment has been given lately to the Code of the Samurai—the Art of Death which makes our soldiers exult in self-sacri-
15 fice; but scarcely any attention has been drawn to Teaism, which represents so much of our Art of Life. . . .

The tearoom is unimpressive in appearance. It is smaller than the smallest
20 of Japanese houses, while the materials

Performing the tea ceremony, a man pours hot water over the powdered green tea he has placed in cups. He will use a bamboo brush to stir the tea, which he will then offer to his guests.

used in its construction are intended to give the suggestion of refined poverty. Yet we must remember that all this is the result of profound artistic foreth-
25 ought, and that the details have been worked out with care perhaps even greater than that expended on the building of the richest palaces and temples. A good tearoom is more costly than an or-
30 dinary mansion, for the selection of its materials, as well as its workmanship, requires immense care and precision. . . .

Again the roji [rō′jē], the garden path
35 which leads from the machiai [mä chē′ī; gate] to the tearoom, signified the first stage of meditation—the passage into self-illumination. The roji was intended to break connection with
40 the outside world, and to produce a fresh sensation conducive to the full enjoyment of aestheticism [appreciation of beauty] in the tearoom itself. One who has trodden this garden path can-
45 not fail to remember how his spirit, as he walked in the twilight of evergreens over the regular irregularities of the stepping stones, beneath which lay dried pine needles, and passed beside
50 the moss-covered granite lanterns, be-

came uplifted above ordinary thoughts. One may be in the midst of a city, and yet feel as if he were in the forest far away from the dust and din of civilization. . . .

Thus prepared the guest will silently approach the sanctuary, and, if a samurai, will leave his sword on the rack beneath the eaves, the tearoom being preeminently the house of peace. Then he will bend low and creep into the room through a small door not more than three feet in height. This proceeding was incumbent on all guests—high and low alike—and was intended to inculcate humility. . . . The host will not enter the room until all the guests have seated themselves and quiet reigns with nothing to break the silence save the note of the boiling water in the iron kettle. The kettle sings well, for pieces of iron are so arranged in the bottom as to produce a peculiar melody in which one may hear the echoes of a cataract muffled by clouds, of a distant sea breaking among the rocks, a rainstorm sweeping through a bamboo forest, or of the soughing of pines on some faraway hill. . . .

However faded the tearoom and the tea-equipage may seem, everything is absolutely clean. Not a particle of dust will be found in the darkest corner, for if any exists the host is not a tea-master. One of the first requisites of a tea-master is the knowledge of how to sweep, clean, and wash, for there is an art in cleaning and dusting. . . .

In this connection there is a story of Rikiu which well illustrates the ideas of cleanliness entertained by the tea-masters. Rikiu was watching his son Shoan [shō′än] as he swept and watered the garden path. "Not clean enough," said Rikiu, when Shoan had finished his task, and bade him try again. After a weary hour the son turned to Rikiu: "Father, there is nothing more to be done. . . . not a twig, not a leaf have I left on the ground." "Young fool," chided the tea-master, "that is not the way a garden path should be swept." Saying this, Rikiu stepped into the garden, shook a tree and scattered over the garden gold and crimson leaves, scraps of the brocade of autumn! What Rikiu demanded was not cleanliness alone, but the beautiful and the natural also. . . .

The tearoom is absolutely empty, except for what may be placed there temporarily to satisfy some aesthetic mood. Some special art object is brought in for the occasion, and everything else is selected and arranged to enhance the beauty of the principal theme. . . .

The simplicity of the tearoom and its freedom from vulgarity make it truly a sanctuary from the vexations of the outer world. There and there alone can one consecrate himself to undisturbed adoration of the beautiful. In the sixteenth century the tearoom afforded a welcome respite from labor to the fierce warriors and statesmen engaged in the unification and reconstruction of Japan.

## Discussing the Reading

1. What is the purpose of the tea ceremony? Are there any similar rituals in Western culture?

2. What is your definition of art? Is the tea ceremony an art form? Why or why not?

### CRITICAL THINKING
### Making Inferences

The Japanese tea ceremony has been performed with the same rituals for hundreds of years. What inferences can you make about what the Japanese value in this cultural tradition? How would you characterize the Japanese sense of beauty?

# The Dialogue of the Sorcerer-Kings

**TIME FRAME**
*Early 13th century*

**GEOGRAPHIC SETTING**
*West Africa*

At the right is a bronze figure of a horseman of the Benin people of West Africa. This figure, dating from the 16th century, was an altarpiece in an ancestral shrine.

A *griot* [grē'o] is an oral historian in West Africa. Griots were once employed by kings and the wealthy to recount the glorious histories of their dynasties and ancestors. The following excerpts from an oral history of Sundiata [sūn'dē ä'tə], the founder of the empire of Mali [mä'lē] in West Africa, were recorded in the 1950s from one of the last professional griots. In the first excerpt the griot introduces himself and his profession. In the second he describes the manner in which the hero Sundiata and his evil opponent, the sorcerer-king Soumaoro [sü'mä ō'rō], taunt each other on the eve of the climactic battle that will decide who rules Mali.

I am a griot. It is I, Djeli Mamoudou Kouyaté [jel'ē mä'mü dü kü yä'tā], son of Bintou [bin'tü] Kouyaté and Djeli Kedian [ke'dē än] Kouyaté, master in the art of eloquence. Since time immemorial the Kouyatés have been in the service of the Keita [kī'tə] princes of Mali; we are vessels of speech, we are the repositories which harbor secrets many centuries old. The art of eloquence has no secrets for us; without us the names of kings would vanish into oblivion, we are the memory of mankind; by the spoken word we bring to life the deeds and exploits of kings for younger generations. . . .

I teach kings the history of their ancestors so that the lives of the ancients might serve them as an example, for the world is old, but the future springs from the past. . . .

Sundiata went and pitched camp at Dayala [dā'ä lə] in the valley of the Niger. Now it was he who was blocking Soumaoro's road to the south. Up till that time, Sundiata and Soumaoro had fought each other without a declaration of war. One does not wage war without saying why it is being waged. Those fighting should make a declaration of their grievances to begin with. Just as a sorcerer ought not to attack someone without taking him to task for some evil deed, so a king should not wage war

without saying why he is taking up
15 arms.

Soumaoro advanced as far as Krina
[krē′nə], near the village of Dayala on
the Niger and decided to assert his
rights before joining battle. Soumaoro
20 knew that Sundiata also was a sorcerer,
so, instead of sending an embassy, he
committed his words to one of his owls.
The night bird came and perched on the
roof of [Sundiata's] tent and spoke.
25 [Sundiata] in his turn sent his owl to
Soumaoro. Here is the dialogue of the
sorcerer kings:

"Stop, young man. Henceforth I am
the king of Mali. If you want peace, re-
30 turn to where you came from," said
Soumaoro.

"I am coming back, Soumaoro, to re-
capture my kingdom. If you want peace
you will make amends to my allies and
35 return to Sosso [Soumaoro's capital]
where you are the king."

"I am king of Mali by force of arms.
My rights have been established by conquest."

40 "Then I will take Mali from you by
force of arms and chase you from my
kingdom."

"Know, then, that I am the wild yam
of the rocks; nothing will make me leave
45 Mali."

"Know, also that I have in my camp
seven master smiths who will shatter
the rocks. Then, yam, I will eat you."

"I am the poisonous mushroom that
50 makes the fearless vomit."

"As for me, I am the ravenous cock,
the poison does not matter to me."

"Behave yourself, little boy, or you
will burn your foot, for I am the red-hot
55 cinder."

"But me, I am the rain that extin-
guishes the cinder; I am the boisterous
torrent that will carry you off."

"I am the mighty silk-cotton tree that
60 looks from on high on the tops of other
trees."

"And I, I am the strangling creeper
that climbs to the top of the forest
giant."
65 "Enough of this argument. You shall
not have Mali."

"Know that there is not room for two
kings on the same skin, Soumaoro; you
will let me have your place."
70 "Very well, since you want war I will
wage war against you, but I would have
you know that I have killed nine kings
whose heads adorn my room. What a
pity, indeed, that your head should take
75 its place beside those of your fellow
madcaps."

"Prepare yourself, Soumaoro, for it
will be long before the calamity that is
going to crash down upon you and
80 yours comes to an end."

Thus Sundiata and Soumaoro spoke
together. After the war of mouths,
swords had to decide the issue.

## Discussing the Reading

1. Like the herdsman and the blacksmith in Reading 9A, the griot
Kouyaté practiced a traditional
occupation. What function did the
griot serve? Kouyaté was one of
the last professional griots. How
will the skills he practiced and
the role he fulfilled in his community be preserved in the future?

2. In describing the exchange of
insults between Sundiata and
Soumaoro, the griot observed,
"One does not wage war without
saying why it is being waged."
How did the manner in which the
two kings mocked each other
resemble a declaration of war
between modern nations? How
did it differ?

**CRITICAL THINKING**
**Making Decisions**

Who do you think wins "the war
of mouths"? Why?

# In the Palace of Montezuma

**TIME FRAME**

*Early 16th century*

**GEOGRAPHIC SETTING**

*Mexico*

When the conquistadors first encountered the Aztecs in Mexico, the Spanish were welcomed as guests and treated with honor by the Aztec king, Montezuma [mon'tə zü'mə] (1498?–1520). The following is an account by Bernal Díaz [bėr'näl dē'äs] (1498–1560), who accompanied the Spanish conqueror Hernando Cortés [hėr nän'dō côr tez'] (1485–1547) into the Aztec capital, Tenochtitlan [tä nōch'tē tlän'], and later wrote a history of the colony of New Spain. Díaz's book provides one of the few glimpses of Mexico before the Spanish conquest. The Christian conquistadors and the priests that accompanied them viewed the books and records of the Aztecs and other Native American peoples as heathen writings and burned almost all of them.

A bove 300 kinds of dishes were served up for Montezuma's dinner from his kitchen, underneath which were placed pans of porcelain filled
5 with fire, to keep them warm. Three hundred dishes of various kinds were served up for him alone, and above 1,000 for the persons in waiting. He sometimes, but very seldom, accom-
10 panied by the chief officers of his household, ordered the dinner himself, and

At right is a detail of a featherwork shield thought to be the ceremonial parade shield of Montezuma's great uncle, Ahuitzotl [ä' wēt-zōtl], who preceded Montezuma as king of the Aztecs. His name means "Water Beast," and that beast is the subject of the shield. The outlines are marked in gold, showing the beast holding a stone sacrificial knife in its mouth.

At the left on the opposite page is a wooden mask, inlaid with shell and turquoise, representing "Lady Precious Green," the Aztec goddess of flowing water. She is wearing a nose pendent like those worn by Aztec noblewomen, and her braided hair is also typical of Aztec fashion. At the upper right is a painting of an Aztec juggler done in 1528 by the German artist Christoph Weiditz (1500–1559). This juggler was one of the Aztecs taken to Spain by Cortés, where Weiditz saw them at the court of the king of Spain, Charles V.

desired that the best dishes and various kinds of birds should be called over to him. . . .

About this time a celebrated cacique, [kə sēk'; prince], whom we called Tapia [tä'pē ä], was Montezuma's chief steward: he kept an account of the whole of Montezuma's revenue, in large books of paper which the Mexicans call *Amatl* [ä mä'tl]. A whole house was filled with such large books of accounts.

Montezuma had also two arsenals filled with arms of every description, of which many were ornamented with gold and precious stones. These arms consisted in shields of different sizes, sabers, and a species of broadsword, which is wielded with both hands, the edge furnished with flint stones, so extremely sharp that they cut much better than our Spanish swords: further, lances of greater length than ours, with spikes at their end, full one fathom in length, likewise furnished with several sharp flint stones. The pikes are so very sharp and hard that they will pierce the strongest shield, and cut like a razor; so that the Mexicans even shave themselves with these stones. . . .

I will now, however, turn to another subject, and rather acquaint my readers with the skillful arts practiced among the Mexicans: among which I will first mention the sculptors, and the gold and silversmiths, who were clever in working and smelting gold, and would have astonished the most celebrated of our Spanish goldsmiths. . . .

The powerful Montezuma had also a number of dancers and clowns: some danced on stilts, tumbled, and performed a variety of other antics for the monarch's entertainment: a whole quarter of the city was inhabited by these performers, and their only occupation consisted in such like performances. Lastly, Montezuma had in his service great numbers of stonecutters, masons, and carpenters, who were solely employed in the royal palaces. Above all, I must not forget to mention here his gardens for the culture of flowers, trees, and vegetables, of which there were various kinds. In these gardens were also numerous baths, wells, basins, and ponds full of limpid water, which regularly ebbed and flowed. All this was enlivened by endless varieties of small birds, which sang among the trees. Also the plantations of medical plants and vegetables are well worthy of our notice: these were kept in proper order by a large body of gardeners. All the baths, wells, ponds, and buildings were substantially constructed of stonework, as also the theaters where the singers and dancers performed. There were upon the whole so many remarkable things for my observation in these gardens and throughout the whole town, that I can scarcely find words to express the astonishment I felt at the pomp and splendor of the Mexican monarch.

## Discussing the Reading

1. Look back at Reading 9B. Compare the lives of the Aztec king Montezuma and the Mayan king Plumed Serpent.

2. Why does most history seem to be a record of the ruling class? Apply your answer to this reading.

**CRITICAL THINKING**
**Synthesizing Information**

What is the role of prestige in the career of a successful leader? What would Machiavelli (see Reading 12B) think about the display of wealth and splendor in Montezuma's palace? Should leaders of a democratic society such as the United States live in splendor as a way of establishing prestige? Explain.

The watercolors by Francesco Bartoli that span these two pages are three different views of the jeweled pin made by Cellini for Pope Clement VII. The front view, on this page, shows the piece set with emeralds, sapphires, and rubies. The figures shown in the side view were done in low relief and are finely enameled. At the far right is the back of the pin, embossed with Clement's coat of arms.

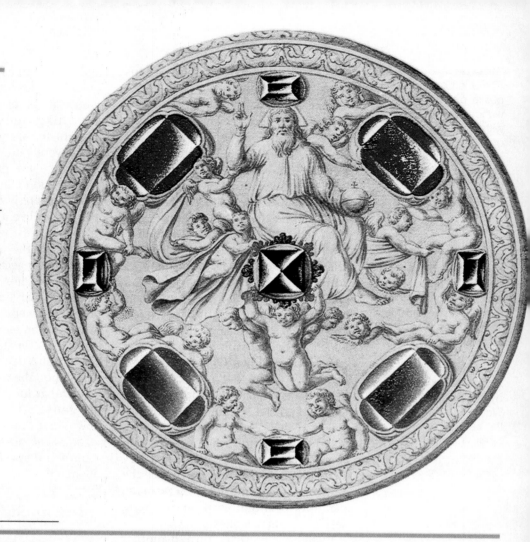

# Benvenuto Cellini— Artist and Rogue

19A

**TIME FRAME**
*Early 16th century*

**GEOGRAPHIC SETTING**
*Italy*

Benvenuto Cellini [ben′və nü′tō chə lē′nē] (1500–1571) was the greatest goldsmith and jeweler of the Renaissance. He worked for dukes, kings, and popes who were anxious to display their wealth in stylish and decorative forms. "They plumed themselves exceedingly when they saw young men of my sort coming to study [the art] in their palaces," Cellini tells us. Cellini was aware of his own genius and proud of his success, so much so that he considered himself above the law. It was typical of the Renaissance that the many brawls, scrapes, and murders in which Cellini was involved were all forgiven so long as

he continued to design and cast beautiful gold, bronze, and jeweled art objects for his patrons. The following excerpts from Cellini's *Autobiography* provide a fascinating view into life in Renaissance Italy. The Pope Clement who was Cellini's patron was Clement VII, pope from 1523 to 1534.

I went on applying myself with the utmost diligence upon the gold work for Pope Clement's button [a pin]. He was very eager to have it, and used to
5 send for me two or three times a week,

in order to inspect it; and his delight in the work was always increased. Often would he rebuke and scold me, as it were, for the great grief in which my
10 brother's loss had plunged me [Cellini's brother had recently been killed in a street brawl]; and one day, observing me more downcast and out of trim than was proper, he cried aloud: "Ben-
15 venuto, oh! I did not know that you were mad. Have you only just learned that there is no remedy against death? One would think that you were trying to run after him." When I left the presence,
20 I continued working at the jewel and the dies for the Mint [another job he had been assigned by the Pope]; but I also took to watching the arquebusier [är′kwə bəs′ər; a musketeer] who shot

25 my brother, as though he had been a girl I was in love with. . . .

The fellow lived in a house near . . . the lodging of one of the most fashionable courtesans in Rome, named Si-
30 gnora Antea [sē nyôr′ə än tē′ə]. It had just struck twenty-four, and he was standing at the house door, with his sword in hand, having risen from supper. With great address I stole up to
35 him, holding a large . . . dagger, and dealt him a backhanded stroke, with which I meant to cut his head clean off; but as he turned round very suddenly, the blow fell upon the point of his left
40 shoulder and broke the bone. He sprang up, dropped his sword, half-stunned with the great pain, and took flight. I followed after, and in four steps caught

him up, when I lifted my dagger above his head, which he was holding very low, and hit him in the back exactly at the junction of the nape-bone and the neck. . . .

More than eight days elapsed, and the Pope did not send for me according to his custom. Afterwards he summoned me through his chamberlain, the Bolognese [bō'lō nyēz'; from the city of Bologna in northern Italy] nobleman I have already mentioned, who let me, in his own modest manner, understand that his Holiness knew all, but was very well inclined toward me, and that I had only to mind my work and keep quiet. When we reached the presence, the Pope cast so menacing a glance towards me that the mere look of his eyes made me tremble. Afterwards, upon examining my work, his countenance cleared, and he began to praise me beyond measure, saying that I had done a vast amount in a short time. Then looking me straight in the face, he added: "Now that you are cured, Benvenuto, take heed how you live." I, who understood his meaning, promised that I would. Immediately upon this, I opened a very fine shop, . . . and there I finished the jewel after the lapse of a few months.

## Discussing the Reading

1. What adjectives would you use to describe Cellini's character?

2. Explain the meaning of Pope Clement's two remarks to Cellini (lines 14–19 and 69–70). What kind of man does Clement appear to have been?

**CRITICAL THINKING**
**Analyzing Information**

Many readers go to Cellini's *Autobiography* not to learn about Cellini so much as to learn about his time. From the passage you have read, analyze the value of the *Autobiography* as a commentary on his period.

# Michelangelo and His Patrons

**TIME FRAME**
*16th century*

**GEOGRAPHIC SETTING**
*Italy*

Probably the greatest and most famous sculptor and painter of the Renaissance was Michelangelo [mī'kə lan'jə lō] (1475–1564). He strove for perfection, so much so that his friend and first biographer Giorgio Vasari [jôr'jō vä zä'rē] (1511–1574) claimed that "shortly before [Michelangelo's] death he burned a large number of designs, sketches, and cartoons [preliminary drawings for paintings] so that none might see the labors he endured in his resolution to achieve perfection." Despite the fame and recognition achieved even during his lifetime, however, Michelangelo had to endure the criticism and harassment of the people who hired him to create his great works of art. The following two incidents told by Vasari relate to two of Michelangelo's greatest works: the statue of David in Florence and the painting of the ceiling of the Sistine Chapel in Rome. The Piero Soderini [pyā'rō sō'də rē'nē] (1452–1522) mentioned by Vasari was a Florentine statesman. The Pope was Julius II, pope from 1503 to 1513.

W hen he saw the [finished statue of] David in place [in the main square in Florence] Piero Soderini was delighted; but while Michelangelo was retouching it, he [Soderini] remarked that he thought the nose was too thick. Michelangelo, noticing that [Soderini] was standing beneath the Giant and that from where he was he could not see the figure properly, to satisfy him climbed on the scaffolding by the shoulders, seized hold of a chisel in his left hand, together with some of the marble dust lying on the planks, and as he tapped lightly with the chisel let the dust fall little by little, without altering anything. Then he looked down at [Soderini], who had stopped to watch, and said:

"Now look at it."

"Ah, that's much better," replied Soderini. "Now you've really brought it to life."

And then Michelangelo climbed down, feeling sorry for those critics who talk nonsense in the hope of appearing well informed.

An interior view of the Sistine Chapel appears above, showing Michelangelo's *Last Judgment* on the altar wall. On the right is the Libyan Sibyl, one of the most famous figures of the Sistine ceiling. The sibyls [sib'əlz] were ten prophetesses in Classical mythology who were associated with different places in the ancient world.

One day while working on the Sistine Chapel ceiling, Michelangelo asked the Pope's permission to go to Florence for the feast day of St. John and wanted some money from him for the purpose, and the Pope said:

"Well, what about this chapel? When will it be finished?"

"When I can, Holy Father," said Michelangelo.

Then the Pope struck Michelangelo with a staff he was holding and repeated:

"When I can! When I can! What do you mean? I will soon make you finish it."

However, after Michelangelo had gone back to his house to prepare for the journey to Florence, the Pope immediately sent his chamberlain, Cursio [cürs'ē ō], with five hundred crowns to calm him down, as he was afraid that he would react in his usual unpredictable way; and the chamberlain made excuses for his holiness, explaining that such treatment was meant as a favor and a mark of affection. Then Michelangelo, because he understood the Pope's nature and, after all, loved him dearly, laughed it off, seeing that everything [contributed] to his profit and advantage and that the Pope would do anything to keep his friendship.

## Discussing the Reading

1. What was Michelangelo's response to criticism in each of the two incidents related by Vasari? Taken together, what do these two episodes suggest about Michelangelo's character?

2. A patron is someone who gives financial support to an artist. Does this financial support entitle a patron to impose conditions on an artist? Why (and what kind of conditions) or why not?

### CRITICAL THINKING
### Analyzing Comparisons

Compare Pope Clement's relationship to Cellini with Pope Julius's to Michelangelo. Consider the relationship both from the patron's side and the artist's.

# The Portuguese Reach India

# 20A

**TIME FRAME**
*Late 15th century*

**GEOGRAPHIC SETTING**
*India*

The goal of the 15th- and 16th-century European explorers was really not to discover a New World but to reach India and the Spice Islands of the East Indies. There they hoped to buy the luxury goods of the East—spices, precious metals, and silks—and sell them back in Europe for large profits. Of course to buy these goods Europeans needed things to exchange with merchants of the East. As demonstrated in the following excerpt from the log of a sailor who accompanied the Portuguese explorer Vasco da Gama (väs'cō də gä'mə] (1469?–1524) on his first successful voyage to India (1497–1499), the Portuguese did not have items that interested the Indians. The Portuguese also found that Muslim merchants, who were already bringing oriental goods to Europe for a great profit, did all they could to prevent the newcomers from breaking their monopoly of trade with the East.

On Sunday [May 20, 1498] we found ourselves close to some mountains, and when we were near enough for the pilot to recognize them he told us that they were above Calecut [kal'ə cut; or Kozhikode, a seaport in

At the right is a picture of Vasco da Gama, taken from a 16th-century manuscript. Da Gama's voyage opened the first all-water trade route between Europe and Asia. On his return from India, Da Gama was given the title "Admiral of the Sea of India" by King Manuel of Portugal.

southwestern India], and that this was the country we desired to go to. . . .

On the following day [some] . . .
10 boats came again alongside, when the captain-major sent one of the [crew] . . . to Calecut, and those with whom he [the crew-member] went took him to two Moors [Muslims] from Tunis, who
15 could speak Castilian [Spanish] and Genoese [Italian]. The first greeting that he received was in these words: "May the Devil take thee! What brought you hither?" They asked what he sought so
20 far away from home, and he told them that we came in search of Christians and of spices. . . .

On Tuesday [May 29] the captain got ready the following things to be sent to
25 the king, viz., twelve pieces of *lambel* [striped cloth], four scarlet hoods, six hats, four strings of coral, a case containing six wash-hand basins, a case of sugar, two casks of oil, and two of
30 honey. And as it is the custom not to send anything to the king without the knowledge of the Moor, his [agent], and of the [governor], the captain informed them of his intention. They came, and
35 when they saw the present they laughed at it, saying that it was not a thing to offer to a king, that the poorest merchant from Mecca, or any other part of India, gave more, and that if he wanted
40 to make a present it should be in gold, as the king would not accept such things. When the captain heard this he grew sad, and said that he had brought no gold, that, moreover, he was no mer-

chant, but an ambassador; . . . and that if King Camolim [kam'ō ləm] would not accept these things he would send them back to the ships. Upon this they declared that they would not forward his presents, nor consent to his forwarding them himself. When they had gone there came certain Moorish merchants, and they all depreciated the present which the captain desired to be sent to the king.

When the captain saw that they were determined not to forward his present, he said that as they would not allow him to send his present to the palace he would go to speak to the king, and would then return to the ships. They approved of this. . . .

The king then said that he [the captain] had told him that he came from a very rich kingdom, and yet had brought him nothing; that he had also told him that he was the bearer of a letter, which had not yet been delivered. To this the captain rejoined that he had brought nothing, because the object of his voyage was merely to make discoveries, but that when other ships came he would then see what they brought him; as to the letter, it was true that he had brought one, and would deliver it immediately.

The king then asked what it was he had come to discover: stones or men? If he came to discover men, as he said, why had he brought nothing?

The king then asked what kind of merchandise was to be found in his country. The captain said there was much corn, cloth, iron, bronze, and many other things. . . . The king said . . . he might . . . land his merchandise, and sell it to the best advantage.

Five days afterwards [on June 7] the captain sent word to the king that, although . . . he had landed his merchandise as he had been ordered, . . . the Moors only came to depreciate

it. . . . The Moors no longer visited the house where the merchandise was, but they bore us no good will, and when one of us landed they spat on the ground, saying: "Portugal, Portugal." Indeed from the very first they had sought means to take and kill us.

. . . We were well aware that the Moors of the place, who were merchants from Mecca and elsewhere, and who knew us, could ill digest us. They had told the king that we were thieves, and that if once we navigated to his country, no more ships from Mecca, nor from Quambaye [Cambay, a city in western India, on the Arabian Sea], nor from Imgros [possibly the Strait of Hormuz, which separates the Persian Gulf from the Arabian Sea], nor from any other part, would visit him. They added that he would derive no profit from this [trade with Portugal] as we had nothing to give, but would rather take away, and that thus his country would be ruined. They moreover, offered rich bribes to the king to capture and kill us, so that we should not return to Portugal.

## Discussing the Reading

1. What error in judgment did the Portuguese make?

2. How did the Muslims attempt to keep the Portuguese out of India?

3. What might have been King Camolim's reason for allowing the Portuguese to stay rather than taking the Muslims' bribes and having the Portuguese killed?

**CRITICAL THINKING**
**Making Hypotheses**

In this account India seems a prosperous—even wealthy— country. Why is it so poor today? What reasons can you offer for this apparent reversal of India's economic position?

# The Financial Importance of Overseas Trade

**TIME FRAME**
*Late 16th century*

**GEOGRAPHIC SETTING**
*Northwestern Europe*

Within 100 years of the discoveries of overseas routes to Asia and the New World, European nations were competing for the trade. Scholars today believe that the profits made from the overseas trade in the 16th and 17th centuries were essential for fueling the expansion of capitalism in Europe and ultimately the Industrial Revolution. Financial houses valued information on overseas trade so much that some hired agents with instructions to pass on any news they learned. Below are examples of such "newsletters" sent to the Fugger [fŭg′ər] Bank of Augsburg, Germany.

## Amsterdam, 24 July 1599

Out of the eight Dutch ships which left fourteen and a half months ago for India to obtain spices, four arrived here this week. They are richly
5 laden. Their most important consignment is nearly three hundred loads of pepper, which should come to over four thousand packets. The remaining cargo consists of other kinds of spices, such as
10 cloves, nutmeg, cinnamon, etc. . . . This is considered here as great tidings, and much wonder is expressed that they should have taken such a short time over the journey. It took them seven
15 months to make the East Indies and they lay two months in Banca [an island off Sumatra]. There they procured all

The painting on the left shows the German banker Jacob Fugger and his bookkeeper in the Fugger counting house. The 17th-century etching above shows Dutch ships unloading merchandise.

their cargo, and have returned in five and a half months. Never have the Portuguese accomplished such a journey.

The Indians of Banca traded with them in most friendly spirit, and the Dutch paid the inhabitants of Banca for all the damage they had caused them three years before. In the meantime, the Portuguese attacked the town of Banca, but with the help of the Dutch, the Indians have killed eight hundred of these and captured the rest with the ships. Whereas the Dutch have succeeded so greatly in this sea journey they will undertake others. . . .

These ships are valued at three hundred thousand Flemish pounds. They will make yearly a great trade in spices and cause many others to alter their course. The Dutch States wish to go out again to India with these ships and to send an envoy to the King of Banca. They will never relinquish this desire unless the King of Spain prevents them by force.

**Antwerp, 22 October 1599**

Letters from Amsterdam report that a Dutch ship, which had sailed with thirty-six other ships from the Can-aries to India, had separated from these and joined two English pirates in robbing a few ships in the Spanish Main. This ship made fast in Texel, which is not far from Amsterdam, but it is not known as yet what goods it has brought. brought. Two Dutch ships have likewise called at Emden with fifteen hundred cases of sugar. Three other ships are expected from Brazil. Dutch navigation to the Indies is becoming ever greater, which will cause the Portuguese heavy damage in their trade.

---

## Discussing the Reading

1. Which countries were competing for overseas trade routes? How had the position of the Portuguese changed from that reflected in Reading 20A?

2. Identify the commodities that were traded. Why were they in demand in Europe?

**CRITICAL THINKING**
**Making Decisions**

If you were a German financier in 1599, would you have recommended investing in the Dutch shipping company that controlled trade with Banca? Why or why not? Consider the risks and the potential for profit.

---

# Martin Luther Makes His Stand                      21A

**TIME FRAME**
*16th century*

**GEOGRAPHIC SETTING**
*Germany*

Martin Luther (1483–1546) was called before Holy Roman Emperor Charles V in the German town of Worms in 1521 to defend his religious writings. In those days the emperor had the right to execute anyone the pope had excommunicated from the Church, and Luther knew that he risked being burned at the stake if he did not admit his writings were wrong. The following is his final statement of defense before the emperor.

Most serene emperor, most illustrious princes, most clement lords, obedient to the time set for me yesterday evening, I appear before you, beseeching you, by the mercy of God, that your most serene majesty and your most illustrious lordships may deign to listen graciously to this my cause— which is, as I hope, a cause of justice and of truth. If through my inexperience I have either not given the proper titles to some, or have offended in some manner against court customs and etiquette, I beseech you to kindly pardon me, as a man accustomed not to courts but to the cells of monks. I can bear no other witness about myself but that I have taught and written up to this time with simplicity of heart, as I had in view only the glory of God and the sound instruction of Christ's faithful.

Most serene emperor, most illustrious princes, concerning those questions proposed to me yesterday on behalf of your serene majesty, whether I acknowledged as mine the books enumerated and published in my name and whether I wished to persevere in their defense or to retract them, I have given to the first question my full and complete answer, in which I still persist and shall persist forever. These books are mine and they have been published in my name by me. . . .

[A] group of my books attacks the papacy and the affairs of the papists as those who both by their doctrines and very wicked examples have laid waste the Christian world with evil that affects the spirit and the body. For no one can deny or conceal this fact, when the experience of all and the complaints of everyone witness that through the decrees of the pope and the doctrines of men the consciences of the faithful have been most miserably entangled, tortured, and torn to pieces. Also, property and possessions, especially in this illustrious nation of Germany, have been devoured by an unbelievable tyranny and are being devoured to this time without letup and by unworthy means. . . . If, therefore, I should have retracted these writings, I should have done nothing other than to have added strength to this [papal] tyranny and I should have opened not only windows but doors to such great godlessness. . . . Good God! What a cover for wickedness and tyranny I should have then become. . . .

From these remarks I think it is clear that I have sufficiently considered and weighed the hazards and dangers, as well as the excitement and dissensions aroused in the world as a result of my teachings, things about which I was gravely and forcefully warned yesterday. . . .

Since then your serene majesty and your lordships seek a simple answer, I will give it in this manner, neither horned nor toothed: Unless I am convinced by the testimony of the Scriptures or by clear reason (for I do not

The portrait of Martin Luther below is an engraving by the German artist Lucas Cranach the Younger (1515–1586).

trust either in the pope or in councils alone, since it is well known that they have often erred and contradicted themselves), I am bound by the Scriptures I
80 have quoted and my conscience is captive to the Word of God. I cannot and I will not retract anything, since it is neither safe nor right to go against conscience.

85 I cannot do otherwise, here I stand, may God help me, Amen.

## Discussing the Reading

1. What kind of impression was Luther trying to make at the opening of his statement? Why did he choose to begin this way?

2. What reasons did Luther give for being unwilling to take back his attacks on the papacy?

3. Luther stated that "it is neither safe nor right to go against conscience." Do you agree or disagree with this statement? Why?

**CRITICAL THINKING**
**Analyzing Information**

Compare this sample of Luther's thought with that of Abelard's in Reading 11B and decide which is the more radical theologian.

# Peter the Great Reforms Fashion

21B

**TIME FRAME**
*17th-18th century*

**GEOGRAPHIC SETTING**
*Russia*

Tsar Peter the Great (1672–1725) undertook far-reaching reforms in Russia. He built a strong modernized army and introduced western technology and industry to Russia. He also tried to reform the thinking and habits of Russia's people, especially the entrenched aristocracy and clergy. He felt that many of their habits—even their fashions in clothing—restricted their ways of thinking. The following passage from a biography of Peter the Great by an early 18th-century French writer describes some of the changes the tsar tried to enforce.

The tsar labored at the reform of fashions, or more properly speaking, of dress. Until that time the Russians had always worn long beards,
5 which they cherished and preserved with much care, allowing them to hang down on their bosoms without even cutting the moustache. With these long beards they wore the hair very short,
10 except the ecclesiastics, who, to distinguish themselves, wore it very long. The tsar, in order to reform that custom, ordered that gentlemen, merchants, and other subjects, except priests and
15 peasants, should each pay a tax of one hundred rubles [rü′bəlz; the ruble is the monetary unit of Russia] a year if they wished to keep their beards; the commoners had to pay one kopeck
20 [kō′pek; 100 kopecks equal one ruble] each. Officials were stationed at the gates of the town to collect that tax, which the Russians regarded as an enormous sin on the part of the tsar and as a
25 thing which tended to the abolition of their religion.

These insinuations, which came from the priests, occasioned the publication of many pamphlets in Moscow, where
30 for that reason alone the tsar was regarded as a tyrant and a pagan; and there were many old Russians who, after having their beards shaved off,

saved them preciously, in order to have
35 them placed in their coffins, fearing that
they would not be allowed to enter
heaven without their beards. As for the
young men, they followed the new
custom with the more readiness as it
40 made them appear more agreeable to
the fair sex.

From the reform in beards we may
pass to that of clothes. Their garments,
like those of the Orientals, were very
45 long, reaching to the heel. The tsar
issued an ordinance abolishing the cos-
tume, commanding all the boyars
[bō yärz'; nobles] and all those who
had position at the court to dress after
50 the French fashion, and likewise to
adorn their clothes with gold or silver
according to their means.

As for the rest of the people, the following method was employed. A suit of
55 clothes cut according to the new fashion
was hung at the gate of the city, with a
decree enjoining upon all except peasants to have their clothes made on this
model, under penalty of being forced to
60 kneel and have all that part of their garments which fell below the knee cut off,
or pay [twenty kopecks] every time they
entered the town with clothes in the old
style. Since the guards at the gates exe-
65 cuted their duty in curtailing the garments in a sportive spirit, the people
were amused and readily abandoned
their old dress, especially in Moscow
and its environs, and in the town which
70 the tsar oftenest visited.

The dress of the women was
changed, too. English hair dressing was
substituted for the caps and bonnets
hitherto worn; bodices, stays, and
75 skirts, for the former undergarment. . . .

In the cartoon below on the left, Peter the Great is shown trimming the beard of a Russian boyar [bō yär'], or noble. The portrait of Peter in battle armor at the right is by his court painter Louis Caravacque.

The same ordinance also provided that in the future women, as well as men, should be invited to entertainments such as weddings, banquets, and
80 the like, where both sexes should mingle in the same hall as in Holland and England. It was likewise added that these entertainments should conclude with concerts and dances, but that only
85 those should be admitted who were dressed in English costumes. His Majesty set the example in all these changes.

## Discussing the Reading

1. What methods did Peter use to encourage the changes he wanted made? Which of these methods do you think was most offensive to his subjects? Why? Which was the least offensive?

2. Why did seemingly superficial changes in clothing and hairstyles impact so strongly on Russian society?

**CRITICAL THINKING**
**Analyzing Comparisons**

Compare the reforms made by Peter the Great with those made by Lycurgus in Sparta (see Reading 4A). Consider the kinds of reforms made, the purpose for the reforms, and the effects the reforms had on the two societies.

# Galileo Defends Scientific Observation

## 22A

**TIME FRAME**
*Early 17th century*

**GEOGRAPHIC SETTING**
*Italy*

The remapping of the world that took place as a result of the voyages of Renaissance explorers was accompanied by attempts to remap the heavens as well. The theory of the Polish astronomer Nicolaus Copernicus [kə pėr′nə kəs] (1473–1543) that the sun, rather than the earth, was the center of the universe, overturned established belief and was condemned by the Church. Support for

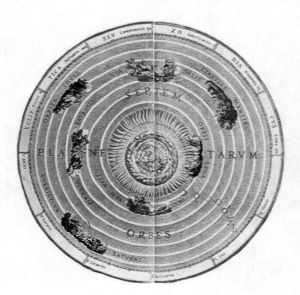

the Copernican theory, however, came from the Italian astronomer and mathematician Galileo [gal'ə lā'ō] (1564–1642), who as a result of his observations with the newly developed telescope was convinced that Copernicus was right and that the earth and the other planets as well all revolved around the sun. In 1615 he wrote the following letter to his friend the Grand Duchess Christina, mother of his pupil and patron Cosimo II, Grand Duke of Tuscany, defending his and Copernicus's ideas against the attacks of the Church.

S ome years ago, as Your Serene Highness well knows, I discovered in the heavens many things that had not been seen before our own age. The nov-
5 elty of these things, as well as some consequences which followed from them in contradiction to the physical notions commonly held among academic philosophers, stirred up against me no
10 small number of professors—as if I had placed these things in the sky with my own hands in order to upset nature and overturn the sciences. They seemed to forget that the increase of known truths
15 stimulates the investigation, establishment, and growth of the arts; not their diminution or destruction.

Showing a greater fondness for their own opinions than for truth, they
20 sought to deny and disprove the new things which, if they had cared to look for themselves, their own senses would have demonstrated to them. To this end they hurled various charges and pub-
25 lished numerous writings filled with vain arguments, and they made the grave mistake of sprinkling these with passages taken from places in the Bible which they had failed to understand
30 properly, and which were ill-suited to their purposes.

. . . Men who were well grounded in astronomical and physical science were persuaded as soon as they received my

35 first message. There were others who denied [my observations] or remained in doubt only because of their novel and unexpected character, and because they had not yet had the opportunity to see
40 for themselves. These men have by degrees come to be satisfied. But some, besides allegiance to their original error, possess I know not what fanciful interest in remaining hostile not so
45 much toward the things in question as toward their discoverer. No longer being able to deny them, these men now take refuge in obstinate silence, but being more than ever exasperated by
50 that which has pacified and quieted other men, they divert their thoughts to other fancies and seek new ways to damage me. . . .

They go about invoking the Bible,
55 which they would have minister to their deceitful purposes. Contrary to the sense of the Bible and the intention of the holy [Church] Fathers, if I am not mistaken, they would extend such
60 authorities until even in purely physical matters—where faith is not involved— they would have us altogether abandon reason and the evidence of our senses in favor of some biblical passage, though
65 under the surface meaning of its words this passage may contain a different sense.

I hope to show that I proceed with much greater piety than they do, when I
70 argue not against condemning this book [by Copernicus], but against condemning it in the way they suggest— that is, without understanding it, weighing it, or so much as reading it.
75 For Copernicus never discusses matters of religion or faith, nor does he use arguments that depend in any way upon the authority of sacred writings which he might have interpreted erroneously. He
80 stands always upon physical conclusions pertaining to the celestial motions, and deals with them by astro-

The two diagrams on the opposite page, produced in 1660, show conflicting views on the structure of the solar system. The one on the left shows the traditional arrangement, with the earth at the center, surrounded by the orbits of the sun, moon, and other planets. The diagram on the right shows the solar system as described by Copernicus, with the sun at the center.

nomical and geometrical demonstrations, founded primarily upon sense
experiences and very exact observations. He did not ignore the Bible, but he

knew very well that if his doctrine were
proved, then it could not contradict the
Scriptures when they were rightly
understood.

## Discussing the Reading

1. Review Reading 11B. How would Abelard have reacted to Galileo's arguments? How would St. Bernard?

2. Why did Galileo stress (in lines 75–90) that Copernicus had not based his theory on arguments from Scripture?

**CRITICAL THINKING**
**Identifying Assumptions**

What assumptions about the relative values of physical evidence and Scriptural authority did Galileo make in this passage?

# Harvey Discovers the Circulation of the Blood

22B

**TIME FRAME**
*Early 17th century*

**GEOGRAPHIC SETTING**
*England*

One of the 17th-century scientists most committed to the scientific method of observation was William Harvey (1578–1657), an English doctor. His discovery of the motion of the heart and circulation of blood resulted from long years of study, experimentation, and dissection of animals, as described in his own words below. His discoveries were a profound breakthrough for medical science, because previously physicians thought the liver was also a source of blood. The following excerpt from his *Essay on the Motion of the Heart and the Blood* also emphasizes one of the important characteristics of modern science—the need to communicate results to other scientists.

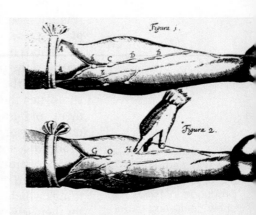

W hen I first gave my mind to vivisections [viv′ə sek′shənz; cutting live animals open for experimenta-
tion] as a means of discovering the
motions and uses of the heart, and
sought to discover these from actual
inspection, and not from the writings of
others, I found the task so truly

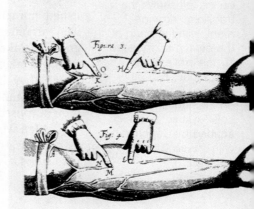

arduous, so full of difficulties, that I was
10 almost tempted to think ... that the
motion of the heart was only to be com-
prehended by God. For I could neither
rightly perceive at first when the systole
[sis′tl ē; contraction of the heart] and
15 when the diastole [dī as′tl ē; dilation of
the heart] took place, nor when and
where dilatation and contraction
occurred, by reason of the rapidity of
the motion, which in many animals is
20 accomplished in the twinkling of an
eye, coming and going like a flash of
lightning; ... My mind was therefore
greatly unsettled, nor did I know what I
should myself conclude, nor what I
25 believe from others. ...

At length, and by using greater and
daily diligence, having frequent
recourse to vivisections, employing a
variety of animals for the purpose, and
30 collating numerous observations, I
thought that I had attained to the truth,
that I should extricate myself and
escape from this labyrinth [maze], and
that I had discovered what I so much
35 desired, both the motion and the use of
the heart and arteries; since which time
I have not hesitated to expose my views
upon these subjects, not only in private
to my friends, but also in public, in my
40 anatomical lectures, after the manner of
the Academy [the school founded by
the Athenian philosopher Plato] of old.

These views, as usual, pleased some
more, others less; some [criticized] and

45 [slandered] me, and laid it to me as a
crime that I had dared to depart from the
precepts and opinion of all anatomists;
others desired further explanations of
the novelties, which they said were both
50 worthy of consideration, and might
perchance be found of signal use. At
length, yielding to the requests of my
friends, that all might be made partici-
pators in my labors, and partly moved
55 by the envy of others, who receiving my
views with uncandid minds and understanding them indifferently, have
essayed to [slander] me publicly, I have
been moved to commit these things to
60 the press, in order that all may be enabled to form an opinion both of me and
my labors. ...

The diagrams on the opposite page were used by William Harvey in his *Essay on the Motion of the Heart and the Blood.*

## Discussing the Reading

1. What problem did Harvey encounter in attempting to deter- mine how blood was circulated in animals? How did he overcome this problem?

2. Why did Harvey decide to publi- cize the results of his research?

**CRITICAL THINKING**
**Making Decisions**

What is your opinion on the use of animals in experiments? Should it be limited to medical research? Should it be outlawed altogether?

# Ottoman Military Power

23A

**TIME FRAME**
*Mid-16th century*

**GEOGRAPHIC SETTING**
*Turkey*

The Ottoman Empire was built on the mil- itary conquest of vast lands. It then con- tinued to be maintained and administered in part by an elite military group, the Jan- issary [jan′ə ser′ē] Corps. This group of soldiers were recruited as small children, regardless of their background, and

raised to be completely loyal to the Ottoman sultan. Other official administra- tors also were selected carefully by the sultan. The following account of the army and the civil service was written by a European who was an ambassador to Constantinople between 1554 and 1562.

The painting above shows the Ottoman sultan Suleiman the Magnificent (1495?–1566) and his army.

At [the Hungarian city of Budapest] I first came across the Janissaries, which is the name they give to their footguards. When they are at their full strength, the Sultan possesses 12,000 of them, scattered throughout his empire, either to garrison the fortresses against the enemy or to protect the Christians and Jews from the violence of the populace. There is no village, town, or city of any size in which there are not some Janissaries . . . .

The Sultan's headquarters were crowded by numerous attendants, including many high officials. All the cavalry of the guard were there . . . and a large number of Janissaries. In all that great assembly no single man owed his dignity to anything but his personal merits and bravery; no one is distinguished from the rest by his birth, and honor is paid to each man according to the nature of the duty and offices which he discharges. . . . The Sultan himself assigns to all their duties and offices, and in doing so pays no attention to wealth or the empty claims of rank, and takes no account of any influence or popularity which a candidate may possess; he only considers merit and scrutinizes the character, natural ability, and disposition of each. Thus each man is rewarded according to his deserts, and offices are filled by men capable of performing them. In Turkey every man has it in his power to make what he will of the position into which he is born and of his fortune in life. Those who hold the highest posts under the Sultan are very often the sons of shepherds and herdsmen, and, so far from being ashamed of their birth, they make it a subject of boasting, and the less they owe to their forefathers and to the accident of their birth, the greater is the pride which they feel. . . . Thus, among the Turks, dignities, offices, and administrative posts are the rewards of ability and merit; those who are dishonest, lazy, and slothful never attain to distinction, but remain in obscurity and contempt. This is why the Turks succeed in all that they attempt and are a dominating race and daily extend the bounds of their rule. Our method is very different; there is no room for merit, but everything depends on birth; considerations of which alone open the way to high official position. . . .

[When on military campaign] the Sultan's store of provisions is opened . . . and just enough food to sustain life is weighed out each day to the Janissaries and the other troops in attendance upon him. . . . Sometimes, too, they have recourse to horseflesh; for in a great army a large number of horses necessarily dies, and any that die in good condition furnish a welcome meal to men who are starving. I may add that men whose horses have died, when the Sultan moves his camp, stand in a long row on the road by which he is to pass with their harness or saddles on their heads, as a sign that they have lost their horses, and implore his help to purchase others. The Sultan then assists them with whatever gift he thinks fit.

All this will show you with what patience, sobriety, and economy the Turks struggle against the difficulties which beset them, and wait for better times.

How different are our soldiers, who on campaign despise ordinary food and expect dainty dishes . . . .

I mentioned that baggage animals are employed on campaign to carry the arms and tents, which mainly belong to the Janissaries. The Turks take the utmost care to keep their soldiers in good health and protected from the inclemency of the weather; against the foe they must protect themselves, but their health is a matter for which the State must provide. . . . As a further protection against cold and rain tents are always carried, in which each man is given just enough space to lie down, so that one tent holds twenty-five or thirty Janissaries. The material for the garments to which I have referred is provided at the public expense. . . .

The armor which is carried is chiefly for the use of the household cavalry, for the Janissaries are lightly armed and do not usually fight at close quarters, but use muskets. . . . [In the Sultan's procession] I saw . . . a long column of Janissaries, scarcely any of whom carried any other arms except their muskets. Almost all wore uniforms of the same shape and color, so that you could recognize them as the slaves or household of the same master. . . .

[On the other hand] there was nothing which the Sultan so much dreaded as that there might be some secret disaffection among the Janissaries, which might break out when it was impossible to apply any remedy. His fears are not entirely groundless. A professional standing army possesses certain great advantages; but it also has serious drawbacks which must be counteracted by special precautions. The chief of these drawbacks is that the sovereign is kept in continual dread of a mutiny, and the soldiers have it in their power to transfer their allegiance to whomsoever they will.

# The First Mughal Emperor

# 23B

**TIME FRAME**
*Early 16th century*

**GEOGRAPHIC SETTING**
*Northern India*

Beyond the Oxus River, the eastern border of Persia, in the vast mountainous region called Turkestan [tėr′kə stan′], was located the small kingdom of Ferghana [fėr gä′nä]. Here in 1473 was born Zahir ud-Din Muhammed, known by his Mongol nickname, *Babur* [bä′ber], "tiger." Babur was the eldest son of the king of Ferghana, and was descended from both the Turkish conqueror Tamerlane and Genghis Khan, founder of the Mongol Empire. His father died while Babur was still a boy, and the young king of Ferghana immediately plunged into the career of military adventuring that would occupy the rest of his life. Although brave, intelligent, energetic, and prudent, Babur experienced many reverses, suffering defeat, exile, and privation. In 1526, with a small force, he invaded and conquered the whole of northern India, the region called Hindustan [hin′də stan′]. He established the Mughal [mü gul′], or "Mongol" dynasty, which would last for over 300 years. Babur was a gifted writer as well as a brilliant soldier. His great literary work is the *Babur-nama* ("Book of Babur"), a frank and vivid account of his life that has been described as the greatest autobiography in Oriental literature. The following excerpt from the *Babur-nama* describes an attempt on his life that took place after Babur's conquest of Hindustan. He had defeated and killed the region's ruler, Sultan Ibrahim

[ib′rä hēm′], at the battle of Panipat. In revenge, the Sultan's mother attempted to have Babur poisoned.

## The Year 1526

A very important incident happened on Friday, the 16th of Rabia-ul-Awal [rä bē′ä ul ä wäl′; third month of the Islamic year], in this
5 year. The circumstances are these:— The mother of Ibrahim, an ill-fated lady, had heard that I had eaten some things from the hand of natives of Hindustan. It happened in this way. Three or four
10 months ago, never having seen any of the dishes of Hindustan, I desired Ibrahim's cooks to be called, and out of fifty or sixty cooks, four were chosen and retained. The lady, having heard the cir-
15 cumstance, sent a person to Etaweh [ā tä′və; a town in northern India] to call Ahmed, the taster, and delivered into the hands of a female slave an ounce of poison, wrapped up in a folded
20 paper, desiring it to be given to the taster Ahmed. Ahmed gave it to a Hindustani cook who was in my kitchen, seducing him with the promise of four districts, and desiring him, by some

Babur's leisure-time activities are portrayed in these two paintings. On the left he is depicted laying out a garden in the Persian style at Kabul in 1508. On the right he is shown dictating to a secretary.

means or other, to throw it into my food. She sent another female slave after the one whom she had desired to carry the poison to Ahmed, in order to observe if the first slave delivered the poison or not. It was fortunate that the poison was not thrown into the pot, it was thrown into the tray. He did not throw it into the pot, because I had strictly enjoined the tasters to watch the Hindustanis, and they had tasted the food in the pot while it was cooking. When they were dishing the meat, my graceless tasters were inattentive, and he threw it upon a plate of thin slices of bread; he did not throw above one half of the poison that was in the paper upon the bread, and put some meat fried in butter upon the slices of bread. If he had thrown it above the fried meat, or into the cooking pot, it would have been still worse; but in his confusion, he spilt the better half of it on the fireplace.

On Friday, when afternoon prayers were past, they dished the dinner. I was very fond of hare, and ate some, as well as a good deal of fried carrot. I was not, however, sensible of any disagreeable taste; I likewise ate a morsel or two of smoke-dried meat, when I felt nausea. The day before, while eating some smoke-dried flesh, I had felt an unpleasant taste in a particular part of it. I ascribed my nausea to that incident. The nausea again returned, and I was seized with so violent a retching, two or three times while the tray was before me, that I had nearly vomited. At last, perceiving that I could not check it, I went out. While on the way my heart rose, and I had again nearly vomited. When I had got outside I vomited a great deal.

I had never before vomited after my food, and not even after drinking wine. Some suspicions crossed my mind. I ordered the cooks to be taken into custody, and desired the meat to be given to a dog, which I directed to be shut up. Next morning about the first watch, the dog became sick, his belly swelled, and he seemed distressed. Although they threw stones at him, and shoved him, they could not make him rise. He remained in this condition till noon, after which he rose and recovered. Two young men had also eaten of this food. Next morning they too vomited much, one of them was extremely ill, but both in the end escaped.

A calamity fell upon me, but I escaped
  in safety,
Almighty God bestowed a new life upon
  me,—
I came from the other world,—
I was again born from my mother's
  womb.

I was broken and dead, but am again
  raised to life;
Now, in the salvation of my life, I recognize the hand of God.

I ordered Muhammed Bakhshi to guard and examine the cooks, and at last all the particulars came to light, as they have been detailed. On Monday, being a court day, I directed all the grandees and chief men, the Begs and Vazirs [və zirz'; begs and vazirs were royal officials] to attend the Diwan [dē wän'; the meeting of an Islamic ruler and his advisers]. I brought in the two men and the two women, who, being questioned, detailed the whole circumstances of the affair in all its particulars. The taster was ordered to be cut to pieces. I commanded the cook to be flayed alive. One of the women was ordered to be tram-pled to death by an elephant; the other I commanded to be shot with a match-lock. The lady I directed to be thrown into custody. She too, pursued by her guilt, will one day meet with due retribution. On Saturday I drank a bowl of milk. I also drank some of the makhtum flower, brayed and mixed in spirits. The milk scoured my inside extremely. Thanks be to God, there are now no remains of illness! I did not fully comprehend before that life was so sweet a thing. The poet says,

Whoever comes to the gates of death,
  knows the value of life.

Whenever these awful occurrences pass before my memory, I feel myself involuntarily turn faint. The mercy of God has bestowed a new life on me, and how can my tongue express my gratitude? Having resolved with myself to overcome my repugnance, I have written fully and circumstantially everything that happened. Although the occurrences were awful, and not to be expressed by the tongue or lips, yet by the favor of Almighty God, other days awaited me, and have passed in happiness and health.

## Discussing the Reading

1. How did Babur conduct his investigation into the attempt on his life?

2. What truth about life did his experience teach Babur?

### CRITICAL THINKING
**Assessing Cause and Effect**

Babur was generally known as a merciful ruler. Considering his reputation for clemency, what might account for the savagery of the punishments he imposed in the poisoning episode?

# The Emperor of China on Ruling

24A

**TIME FRAME**
*Late 17th-early 18th century*

**GEOGRAPHIC SETTING**
*China*

The Manchus [man′chūz] were a nomadic people from Manchuria, the region to the northeast of China. During the 17th century they invaded and conquered China. Kangxi [käng′shē′], who ruled from 1661 to 1722, was the greatest of the Manchu emperors. Intelligent, hardworking, and devoted to duty, he was a brave soldier, an inquisitive scholar, and an able administrator. His character reflected both his nomadic Manchu heritage—he delighted in hunting, for example—and a thorough Chinese education. He did a great deal of writing, which included both official documents and memoranda, as well as letters and poems. These writings provide an extraordinary glimpse into the mind of an emperor of China and his daily activities in governing his vast realm. The following excerpts from Kangxi's writings suggest the emperor's ideas about what makes a good ruler.

Giving life to people and killing people—those are the powers that the emperor has. He knows that administrative errors in government bureaus can be rectified, but that a criminal who has been executed cannot be brought back to life any more than a chopped string can be joined together again. He knows, too, that sometimes people have to be persuaded into morality by the example of an execution. In 1683, after Taiwan had been captured, the court lecturers and I discussed the image of the fifty-sixth hexagram in the *Book of Changes*, "Fire on the Mountain": the calm of the mountain signifies the care that must be used in imposing penalties; the fire moves rapidly on, burning up the grass, like lawsuits that should

Reflecting grandeur and serenity, this portrait of Kangxi is by an unknown 19th-century artist.

be settled speedily. My reading of this was that the ruler needs both clarity and care in punishing: his intent must be to punish in order to avoid the need for further punishing.

Hu Jianjing [hü′jyäng′jēng′] was a subdirector of the Court of Sacrificial Worship whose family terrorized their native area in Jiangsu [jyäng′sü′], seizing people's lands and wives and daughters, and murdering people after falsely accusing them of being thieves. When a commoner finally managed to impeach him, the Governor was slow to hear the case, and the Board of Punishments recommended that Hu be dismissed and sent into exile for three years. I ordered instead that he be executed with his family, and in his native place, so that all the local gentry might learn how I regarded such behavior. Corporal Yambu was sentenced to death for gross corruption in the shipyards; I not only agreed to the penalty but sent guards officer Uge to supervise the beheading, and ordered that all shipyard personnel from generals down to private soldiers kneel down in full armor, and listen to my warning that execution would be their fate as well unless they ended their evil ways. . . .

But apart from such treason cases, when there are men who have to be executed immediately (even if it's spring, when executions should not be carried out), or when one is dealing with men like those who plotted against me in the Heir-Apparent crisis and had to be killed immediately and secretly without trial, I have been merciful where possible. For the ruler must always check carefully before executions, and leave room for the hope that men will get better if they are given the time. In the hunt one can kill all the animals caught inside the circle, but one can't always bear to shoot them as they stand there, trapped and exhausted.

## Eulogy for Governor-General Zhao Hongxie

For forty years you served around Beijing;
Soldiers and people praised your measured goodness
5 I protected and favored you all the way
And all now weep that you have died.

You didn't fear the thugs, you kept the laws,
While you guarded the money,
10 honesty reigned.
Now you are in the underworld but your office remains.
Riding past I think of your insignia— hanging there.

Kangxi, 1722

## Discussing the Reading

1. According to Kangxi, when is execution an appropriate form of punishment? Cite his exact words. Do you agree with Kangxi that the two powers a ruler has are giving life and killing?

2. What did Kangxi want rulers to consider before they order executions? Are these the only considerations?

3. Based on Kangxi's eulogy, what made Governor-General Zhao Hongxie [jou′ hong′shē′] such an effective civil servant?

**CRITICAL THINKING**
**Synthesizing Information**

How might Kangxi's ideas about what makes a good ruler apply to the United States today? Consider how an increase in the number of executions might affect morality and criminal activity. Do our leaders need to be merciful? How can we "leave room for the hope that men will get better"?

The portrait at the right is of the shogun Tokugawa Ieyasu (1543–1616), who toward the end of his reign began the policy of excluding foreign missionaries from Japan that would culminate twenty years later in the "Closed Country" Edict of 1636. The picture at the left, which shows an elephant that was imported by Dutch merchants as a gift for the shogun, is an early example of a Japanese depiction of a European.

# No Japanese May Go Abroad

**TIME FRAME**
*17th century*

**GEOGRAPHIC SETTING**
*Japan*

Christianity was introduced to Japan by priests accompanying the Spanish and Portuguese trading ships in the late 1500s. By the early 1600s the Japanese had become alarmed by the spread of the religion, which undermined an established authority based on Confucian and Buddhist religious values. The Tokugawa [tō kü gä'wä] shoguns therefore banned trade with all foreigners, as decreed by the *Sakoku* [sä kō'kü], or "Closed Country" Edict of 1636. Only one ship per year, a Dutch ship, was allowed to trade at Japan's main foreign port, Nagasaki [nä'gä sä'kē], provided that no foreigner tried to convert any Japanese to Christianity. The large Christian community that had grown up in Nagasaki was persecuted, and many Japanese Christians were crucified.

**The Sakoku,
or "Closed Country" Edict
of June, 1636**

1. No Japanese ships may leave for foreign countries.

2. No Japanese may go abroad secretly. If anybody tries to do this, he will
5 be killed, and the ship and owner(s) will be placed under arrest whilst higher authority is informed.

3. Any Japanese now living abroad who tries to return to Japan will be put
10 to death.

4. If any Kirishitan [Christian] believer is discovered, you two [Nagasaki officials] will make a full investigation.

阿蘭陀船入津圖

In a Japanese painting, many flags fly from a Dutch ship anchored at the harbor of Nagasaki, Japan's main foreign port.

bateren or other criminal foreigners will be imprisoned at Omura as hitherto.

8. Strict search will be made for bateren on all incoming ships.

9. No offspring of Southern Barbarians [Europeans] will be allowed to remain. Anyone violating this order will be killed, and all relatives punished according to the gravity of the offence.

10. If any Japanese have adopted the offspring of Southern Barbarians they deserve to die. Nevertheless, such adopted children and their foster-parents will be handed over to the Southern Barbarians for deportation.

11. If any deportees should try to return or to communicate with Japan by letter or otherwise, they will of course be killed if they are caught, whilst their relatives will be severely dealt with, according to the gravity of the offence.

12. Samurai are not allowed to have direct commercial dealings with either foreign or Chinese shipping at Nagasaki.

5. Any informer(s) revealing the whereabouts of a bateren [Spanish and Portuguese] will be paid 200 or 300 pieces of silver. If any other categories of Kirishitans are discovered, the informer(s) will be paid at your discretion as hitherto.

6. On the arrival of foreign ships, arrangements will be made to have them guarded by ships provided by the Omura clan whilst report is being made to Edo [ā'dō; or Tokyo, the Tokugawa capital], as hitherto.

7. Any foreigners who help the

## Discussing the Reading

1. Why did the Japanese fear the Christian influence on their country? What areas of Japanese culture might the Christians have altered?

2. What did the use of the term "Southern Barbarians" indicate about the Japanese?

3. What factors made Japan well-suited to a policy of isolation? Why was a similar policy less successful for the United States following World War I? Can isolation be a successful policy in today's world?

### CRITICAL THINKING
### Predicting Effects

What results would you expect as a result of this decree? Assess positive and negative results.

# Spanish Attitudes Toward Indians

**TIME FRAME**
*Mid-16th century*

**GEOGRAPHIC SETTING**
*Central America*

The following selection describes Spanish treatment of the Mayas. It was written by a Spanish Franciscan monk, Diego de Landa [dē ā'gō də län'də], who had been sent to convert the Mayas to Christianity. In July of 1562 he himself committed one of the most notorious crimes against Mayan culture: he burned, as the "works of the devil," all the written Mayan manuscripts that he could find. Thus, vast amounts of information about hundreds of years of Mayan culture and history were destroyed in a few moments of religious zeal.

The Indians took the yoke of servitude grievously. The Spaniards held the towns comprising the country well partitioned, but there were some among the Indians who kept stirring them up, and very severe punishments were inflicted in consequence, resulting in the reduction of the population. Several principal men of the province of Cupul [cü pül'] they burned alive, and others they hung. Information being laid against the people of Yobain [yō bä'ēn], a town of the Chels [Mayas], they took the leading men, put them in stocks in a building and then set fire to the house, burning them alive with the greatest inhumanity in the world. I, Diego de Landa, say that I saw a great tree near the village upon the branches of which a captain had hung many women, with their infant children hung from their feet. . . .

The Indians of the provinces of Cochuah [kō'chwə] and Chetumal [chā tü məl'] rose [in rebellion], and the Spaniards so pacified them that from being the most settled and populous it became the most wretched of the whole country. Unheard-of cruelties were inflicted, cutting off their noses, hands, arms, and legs, . . . thrusting the children with spears because they could not go as fast as their mothers. If some of those who had been put in chains fell sick or could not keep up with the rest, they would cut off their heads among the rest rather than stop to unfasten them. They also kept great numbers of women and men captive in their service, with similar treatment. . . .

In their defense the Spaniards urge that being so few in numbers they could not have reduced so populous a country save through the fear of such terrible punishments. . . . On the other hand, the Indians were right in defending their liberty and trusting to the valor of their chiefs, and they thought it would so result as against the Spaniards.

They tell of a Spanish crossbowman and an Indian archer, who being both very expert sought to kill each other, but

The 16th-century drawing below shows a Spaniard kicking an Indian.

neither could take the other unawares. The Spaniard feigning to be off guard, 55 put one knee to the ground, whereupon the Indian shot an arrow that entered his hand and going up the arm separated the bones from each other. At the same moment the Spaniard shot his 60 crossbow and struck the Indian in the chest. He, feeling himself mortally wounded, cut a withe [a thin, flexible branch of a willow tree] . . . and hung himself with it that it might not be said 65 that a Spaniard had killed him. Of such instances of valor there are many.

## Discussing the Reading

1. How did the Spanish treat the Mayas? What does this indicate about the attitude the Spanish had towards the Mayas? To what extent did Diego de Landa agree with this attitude and the resulting actions?

2. Reread lines 50–66. What behavior would the Mayas have encouraged by repeating this legend? Can such tales influence behavior? Explain.

3. If you were responsible for justifying the Spanish treatment of the Mayas, what arguments would you use?

**CRITICAL THINKING**
**Synthesizing Information**

What advice would Kangxi (see Reading 24A) offer the Spanish about ruling the Mayas? Would you agree with his recommendations? Why or why not?

# The Souls of American Indians

25B

**TIME FRAME**
*Early 16th century*

**GEOGRAPHIC SETTING**
*Cuba*

Bartolomé de Las Casas [bär tō'lō mā' dä läs kä'säs] (1474–1566) took part in the Spanish conquest of Cuba in 1513. He was shocked by the Spanish treatment of the American Indians and argued aggressively with the king of Spain that such treatment was not worthy of a Christian monarch. He theorized that the American Indians had souls (something many Spaniards denied) and that God and the Pope had placed them under Spain's authority to care for them. Therefore, Indians should be treated well and taught Christianity, two goals which the *encomienda* and *repartimiento* systems were not set up to accomplish. The *encornienda* [en'kō mē en'də] and *repartimiento* [rä pär'tē myen'tō] were systems in which grants of land, including the right to the forced labor of the Indians living on it, were made to Spaniards. The Spanish king, Charles V, tried to imple-

ment Las Casas's ideas, but resistance from Spanish settlers meant reforms only partly succeeded. The following excerpts from Las Casas's *General History of the Indies* contain some of his ideas.

I t had been written that these peoples of the Indies, lacking human governance and ordered nations, did not have the power of reason to govern themselves—which was inferred only from 5 their having been found to be gentle, patient, and humble. It has been implied that God became careless in creating so immense a number of rational souls and let human nature, 10 which He so largely determined and provided for, go astray in the almost infinitesimal part of the human lineage which they comprise. From this it follows that they have all proven themselves unsocial and therefore monstrous, contrary to the natural bent of all peoples of the world; . . . [But] not only have [the Indians] shown themselves to be very wise peoples and possessed of lively and marked understanding, prudently governing and providing for their nations (as much as they can be nations, without faith in or knowledge of the true God) and making them prosper in justice; but they have equalled many diverse nations of the world, past and present, that have been praised for their governance, politics, and customs, and exceed by no small measure the wisest of all these, such as the Greeks and Romans, in adherence to the rules of natural reasons.

**The Indians are as capable as any other nations to receive the Gospel:** Thus it remains stated, demonstrated and openly concluded . . . throughout this book that all these peoples of the Indies possessed—as far as is possible through natural and human means and without the light of faith—nations, towns, villages, and cities, most fully and abundantly provided for. With a few exceptions in varying degrees they lacked nothing, and some were endowed in full perfection for political and social life and for attaining and enjoying that civic happiness which in this world any good, rational, well provided, and happy republic wishes to have and enjoy; for all are by nature of

The savagery of a Spanish massacre of Indians at Cholula is pictured in a painting intended to illustrate Las Casas's *General History of the Indies*.

very subtle, lively, clear, and most capable understanding. . . .

Merely for the sin of idolatry or for any other sin, however enormous, grave, and heinous, . . . the unfaithful, particularly those whose lack of faith is simple ignorance, *cannot be punished by any judge in the world*—unless it be a case of those who directly impede the propagation of the faith. . . .

The rulers of Castile are obliged by divine law to see that the faith of Christ is preached in the form which the Son of God left established in His Church. . . . To subject them first by warlike means is a form and procedure contrary to the law, gentle yoke, easy burden, and gentleness of Jesus Christ. . . .

Satan could not have invented any more effective pestilence with which to destroy the whole new world, to consume and kill off all its people, and to depopulate it as such large and populous lands have been depopulated, than the inventions of the *repartimiento* and *encomiendas*, by which those peoples [the Indians] were divided and assigned to Spaniards as if to all the devils put together, or like herds of cattle delivered to hungry wolves. (This means would have sufficed to depopulate the whole world.) By the *encomienda* or *repartimiento*, which was the cruelest form of tyranny and the one most worthy of hell-fire that could have been invented, all those peoples are prevented from receiving the Christian faith and religion, being held night and day by their wretched and tyrannical overlords, the Spaniards, in the mines, at personal labors, and under incredible tributes; forced to carry loads one and two hundred leagues as if they were beasts or worse; and with clerics who preach the faith and give the Indians instruction and a knowledge of God persecuted and driven out of the Indian villages, leaving no witnesses to the acts of violence, cruelties, and continual robberies and murders. Because of the *encomiendas* and *repartimiento* the Indians have suffered and still suffer continual tortures, thefts, and injustices to their persons and to their children, women, and worldly goods. Because of the *encomiendas* and *repartimiento* there have perished in the space of forty-six years (and I was present) more than fifteen million souls without faith or sacraments, and more than three thousand leagues of land have been depopulated. I have been present, as I say, and as long as these *encomiendas* last, I ask that God be a witness and judge of what I say: the power of the monarchs, even were they on the scene, will not suffice to keep all the Indians from perishing, dying off, and being consumed; and in this way a thousand worlds might end, without any remedy.

## Discussing the Reading

1. What was the basis for the Spanish argument that the Indians had no souls? What advantage did this give the Spanish? How did Las Casas challenge their argument?

2. The Spanish denied that the Indians had souls, the Nazis used tattooed numbers instead of names for prisoners in concentration camps, and South Africans prevent blacks from receiving treatment in white hospitals except in emergencies. What do these policies have in common? What is the purpose of such policies?

### CRITICAL THINKING
**Predicting Effects**

Can a society practice unethical or immoral behavior without consequences? What are the possible effects on society? On individuals in that society?

The print on the right, produced in 1656 by the Royalist political opponents of Oliver Cromwell, shows him as a villain engaged in destroying the monarchy (symbolized by the crown and royal coat of arms), the Church of England (symbolized by the Bible), and English law (symbolized by books labeled "Magna Charta" and "Statutes").

# Cromwell Dismisses Parliament

26A

**TIME FRAME**
*Mid-17th century*

**GEOGRAPHIC SETTING**
*London*

The English Civil War (1642–1651) was fought in part to establish the principle that England's elected Parliament really was the law of the land and even kings had to obey it. Oliver Cromwell (1599–1658) was the military and religious leader of the Parliamentary forces. Following the execution of Charles I in 1649, however, he found that working with Parliament was as difficult as the king had found it. In 1653 Cromwell called troops into Parliament, dismissing the members by force, as described in the following excerpt from the memoirs of Edmund Ludlow (1617–1692), one of Cromwell's political opponents. Cromwell then ruled virtually as a dictator until his death in

1658. As a result, many English became disillusioned with rule without a king and were glad to restore the kingship to Charles II after Cromwell's death.

Then calling to Major-General Harrison, who was on the other side of the House [chamber where Parliament met], to come to him, he [Cromwell] told him that he judged the Parliament ripe for a dissolution, and this to be the time of doing it. . . . and suddenly standing up, made a speech, wherein he loaded the Parliament with the vilest reproaches, charging them not to have a heart to do any thing for the public good, to have espoused the corrupt interest of [church officials] and the lawyers, who were the supporters of tyr-

15 anny and oppression, accusing them of an intention to perpetuate themselves in power, . . . and thereupon told them, that the Lord had done with them, and had chosen other instruments for the

20 carrying on [of] his work that were more worthy. This he spoke with so much passion and [confusion] of mind, as if he had been distracted. Sir Peter Wentworth stood up to answer him,

25 and said that this was the first time that ever he had heard such unbecoming language given to the Parliament, and that it was the more horrid in that it came from their servant, and their

30 servant whom they had so highly trusted and obliged: but as he was going on, the General [Cromwell] stepped into the midst of the House, where continuing his distracted language he said,

35 "Come, come, I will put an end to your [foolish talking]"; then walking up and down the House like a madman, and kicking the ground with his feet, he cried out, "You are no Parliament, I say

40 you are no Parliament; I will put an end to your sitting; call them in, call them in:" whereupon the sergeant attending the Parliament opened the doors, and Lieutenant-Colonel Worsley with two

45 files of musketeers entered the House; which Sir Henry Vane observing from his place, said aloud, "This is not honest, yea it is against morality and common honesty." Then Cromwell

50 [began to insult] him, crying out with a loud voice, "O Sir Henry Vane, Sir Henry Vane, the Lord deliver me from Sir Henry Vane." Then looking upon one of the members, he said, "There

55 sits a drunkard"; and giving much reviling language to others, he commanded the mace [a symbol of government authority] to be taken away, saying,

"What shall we do with this bauble?

60 Here, take it away." Having brought all into this disorder, Major-General Harrison went to the Speaker as he sat in the chair, and told him, that seeing things were reduced to this pass, it would not

65 be convenient for him to remain there. The Speaker answered that he would not come down unless he were forced. "Sir," said Harrison, "I will lend you my hand"; and thereupon putting his hand

70 within his, the Speaker came down. Then Cromwell applied himself to the members of the House, who were in number between 80 and 100, and said to them, "It's you that have forced me to

75 this, for I have sought the Lord night and day, that he [should] . . . rather slay me than put me upon the doing of this work." . . . Cromwell having acted this treacherous and impious part, ordered

80 the guard to see the House cleared of all the members, and then seized upon the records that were there . . . and having commanded the doors to be locked up, went away to Whitehall [a royal palace

85 later used as a government building].

## Discussing the Reading

1. What reasons did Cromwell give for dissolving Parliament?

2. What higher authority did Cromwell invoke for dissolving Parliament? Why?

3. Edmund Ludlow was a political opponent of Cromwell's. How is this reflected in his account? How might an account of the same episode by a supporter of Cromwell have differed?

**CRITICAL THINKING**
**Analyzing Comparisons**

Review Reading 12A. Compare King John's character and situation as reported by the monkish chronicler with Cromwell's as reported by Ludlow.

# Almighty God Hath Created the Mind Free

**TIME FRAME**
*Late 18th century*

**GEOGRAPHIC SETTING**
*United States*

Below is Jefferson's design for his tomb. He said that he wished to be remembered for founding the University of Virginia and writing the Declaration of Independence and Virginia's statute for religious freedom.

The Enlightenment was a philosophical movement in 18th-century Europe that emphasized rationalism, intellectual freedom, and freedom from prejudice in social and political activity. In 1791 the new United States government guaranteed religious freedom in the Bill of Rights, but some of the state governments had earlier written such guarantees into their state constitutions. In Virginia, a Bill for Establishing Religious Freedom was written in 1777 by Thomas Jefferson (1743–1826), author of the Declaration of Independence and third President of the United States. Jefferson's own Enlighten-ment principles were well summed up in his famous statement, "I have sworn upon the altar of God, eternal hostility against every form of tyranny over the mind of man." The following excerpts from the Virginia statute for religious freedom begin with a series of assumptions (lines 1–60) that establish the philosophical principles upon which the statute is based. At the conclusion of these comes the actual statement (lines 61–77) of the law guaranteeing religious freedom in Virginia.

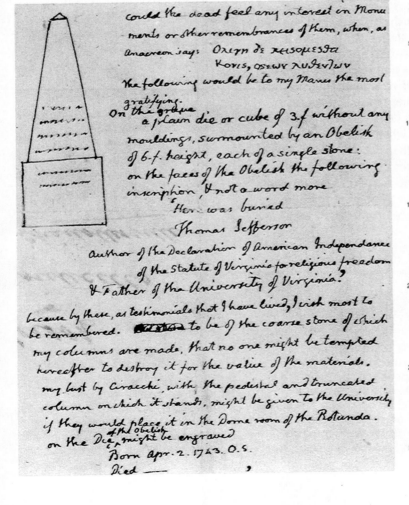

Whereas Almighty God hath created the mind free, that all attempts to influence it by temporal punishments, or burdens, or by civil
5 incapacitations, tend only to beget habits of hypocrisy and meanness, and are a departure from the plan of the holy author of our religion, who being lord both of body and mind, yet chose not to
10 propagate it by coercions on either, as was in his Almighty power to do, that the impious presumption of legislators and rulers, civil as well as ecclesiastical, who, being themselves but fallible and
15 uninspired men, have assumed dominion over the faith of others, setting up their own opinions and modes of thinking as the only true and infallible, and as such endeavoring to
20 impose them on others, hath established and maintained false religions over the greatest part of the world and through all time:

That to compel a man to furnish con-
25 tributions of money for the propagation of opinions which he disbelieves is sinful and tyrannical:

That even the forcing him to support this or that teacher of his own religious
30 persuasion, is depriving him of the com-

fortable liberty of giving his contributions to the particular pastor whose morals he would make his pattern, and whose powers he feels most persuasive
35 to righteousness; and is withdrawing from the ministry those temporary rewards, which proceeding from an approbation of their personal conduct, are an additional incitement to earnest
40 and unremitting labors for the instruction of mankind;

That our civil rights have no dependence on our religious opinions, any more than our opinions in physics or
45 geometry; . . .

That it tends also to corrupt the principles of that *very* religion it is meant to encourage, by bribing, with a monopoly of worldly honors and emoluments,
50 those who will externally profess and conform to it; . . .

And finally, that truth is great and will prevail if left to herself; that she is the proper and sufficient antagonist to
55 error, and has nothing to fear from the conflict unless by human interposition disarmed of her natural weapons, free argument and debate; errors ceasing to be dangerous when it is permitted freely
60 to contradict them.

*We the General Assembly of Virginia do enact* that no man shall be compelled to frequent or support any religious worship, place, or ministry whatso-

65 ever, . . . but that all men shall be free to profess, and by argument to maintain, their opinions in matters of religion, and that the same shall in no wise diminish, enlarge, or affect their civil
70 capacities.

And . . . we are free to declare, and do declare, that the rights hereby asserted are of the natural rights of mankind, and that if any act shall be hereafter passed
75 to repeal the present or to narrow its operation, such act will be an infringement of natural right.

## Discussing the Reading

1. What does Jefferson claim has been the result throughout history of attempts by rulers to impose their religious beliefs on the people they govern?

2. What are Jefferson's objections to a state religion?

3. Review Reading 7B. Compare the views on religious freedom expressed in Asoka's 12th Rock Edict with Jefferson's statute.

**CRITICAL THINKING**
**Making Decisions**

Is it important to have freedom of religion in a society where many people are not religious? Defend your answer.

# The Fall of the Bastille

27A

**TIME FRAME**
*Late 18th century*

**GEOGRAPHIC SETTING**
*Paris*

On July 14, 1789, an armed crowd of Parisian shopkeepers and laborers, looking for weapons and gunpowder, surrounded and stormed the Bastille [ba stēl′], an old fort used as a prison. To the people of France, the Bastille, which had been used for imprisoning without trial religious and political dissidents, rep-

resented the unjust and authoritarian rule of the royal government. As a demonstration of the strength of the people's will, the fall of the Bastille symbolized the rapidly developing revolution. To this day, July 14, "Bastille Day," is celebrated as the beginning of the French Revolution—the "Independence Day" of France.

## Tuesday 14 July

The night of Monday to Tuesday was extremely quiet, apart from the arrest by the citizen militia of some thirty-four unauthorized persons who had plundered and caused a great deal of damage at St. Lazare [sänt′ lä zär′; a district of Paris]; they have been taken into custody.

But a victory of outstanding significance, and one which will perhaps astonish our descendants, was the taking of the Bastille, in four hours or so.

Joyous Parisians celebrate the fall of the Bastille in the print on the right. On the left is the Opéra de la Bastille, a new "people's opera" house near the site of the demolished prison.

First the people tried to enter this fortress by the Rue St.-Antoine [rü′ sänt än twän′], this fortress which no one has ever penetrated against the wishes of this frightful despotism. . . . The treacherous governor [of the Bastille] had put out a flag of peace. So a confident advance was made; a detachment of French Guards [a part of the army that had gone over to the people], with perhaps five to six thousand armed bourgeois [bùr zhwä′; middle class citizens], penetrated the Bastille's outer courtyards, but as soon as some six hundred persons had passed over the first drawbridge, the bridge was raised and artillery fire mowed down several French Guards. . . . A large number of individuals were killed or wounded; but then they rallied and took shelter from the fire; a row of bayonets, fixed in the wall, enabled some brave individual to cut through a post that locked the drawbridge; immediately it fell and they came to the second ditch, near which lay the first victims; meanwhile, they tried to locate some cannon; they attacked from the water's edge through the gardens of the arsenal, and from there made an orderly siege; they advanced from various directions, beneath a ceaseless round of fire. It was a terrible scene. . . . About three o'clock they captured the overseer of the gunpowder store, whose uniform made them mistake him for the Governor of the Bastille; he was manhandled and taken to the town, where he was recognized and set free. The fighting grew steadily more intense; the citizens had become hardened to the fire; from all directions they clambered onto the roofs or broke into the rooms; as soon as an enemy appeared among the turrets on the tower, he was fixed in the sights of a hundred guns and mown down in an instant; . . . the fury was at its height; people bravely faced death and every danger; women, in their eagerness, helped us to the utmost; even the children, after the discharge of fire from the fortress, ran here and there picking up the bullets and shot; [and so the Bastille fell and the governor was captured]. . . . Serene and blessed liberty, for the first time, has at last been introduced into this abode of horrors, this frightful refuge of monstrous despotism and its crimes.

Meanwhile, they [the victors] get ready to march [to the city square]; they 75 leave amidst an enormous crowd; the applause, the outbursts of joy, the insults, the oaths hurled at the treacherous prisoners of war; everything is confused; cries of vengeance and of 80 pleasure issue from every heart; the conquerors, glorious and covered in honor, carry their arms and the spoils of the conquered, the flags of victory, the militia mingling with the soldiers of the 85 fatherland, the victory laurels offered them from every side,—all this created a frightening and splendid spectacle. On arriving at the square, the people, anxious to avenge themselves, allowed nei- 90 ther De Launay [dù lô′nā; the governor of the Bastille] nor the other officers to reach the place of trial; they seized them from the hands of their conquerors, and trampled them underfoot one after the 95 other. De Launay was struck by a thousand blows, his head was cut off and hoisted on the end of a pike with blood streaming down all sides. . . . This glo-

rious day must amaze our enemies, and 100 finally usher in for us the triumph of justice and liberty. In the evening, there were celebrations.

## Discussing the Reading

1. If you had read this newspaper article at the time it appeared, would you have considered this event to be the most important that had occurred in your life? Why or why not? What factors might have affected you?

2. Did De Launay receive justice? What is the difference between revolution and mob rule? Which was this? Defend your answer.

### CRITICAL THINKING
### Evaluating Sources of Information

Was the writer of this account biased? What was his point of view? Use quotes from the article to support your answer. Is this account a primary or secondary historical source?

# The Beginnings of Mexican Independence

27B

**TIME FRAME**
*Early 19th century*

**GEOGRAPHIC SETTING**
*Mexico*

In 1810 the priest Miguel Hidalgo [mē gel′ ē däl′gō] (1753–1811) demanded Mexican independence from Spain in a speech to a large crowd in the town of Dolores. The *Grito de Dolores* [grē′tō dā dō lō′res; "Cry of Dolores"], as his speech was called, said in part: "My children: a new dispensation comes to us today. Will you receive it? Will you free yourselves? Will you recover the lands stolen three hundred years ago from your forefathers by the hated Spaniards? We must act at once. . . . Will you not defend your religion and your rights as true patriots? Long live our Lady of

Guadalupe [gwä′dä lü′pā; the Blessed Virgin as patroness of Mexico]! Death to bad government!" Hidalgo soon found he had to do more to persuade people to follow him into a war of independence. In late 1810 he issued the following proclamation abolishing slavery and heavy taxes in order to appeal to Indians, blacks, and mestizos [me stē′zōs; persons of mixed descent, especially the children of a Spaniard and an American Indian]. In fact this appeal to the masses alienated Hidalgo's creole supporters and was in part a cause of the ultimate failure of Hidalgo's rebellion.

### Decree of Hidalgo,
### Given in Guadalajara, Jalisco,
### in December 1810

From the happy moment that the valiant American nation took up arms to shake off the heavy yoke that has oppressed it for three centuries, one
5 of the principal objectives has been to extinguish such duties that cannot advance its fortune, especially those which in these critical circumstances do not well serve that end or provide for the
10 real need of the kingdom in meeting the costs of the struggle, so therefore there is now put forward here the most urgent remedy in the following declarations:

1. That all owners of slaves shall give
15 them their freedom before the end of ten days, under penalty of death, which shall be applied to those who violate this article.

2. That from now on the collection of
20 tributes according to caste [race] shall cease, as shall exactions that are demanded of the Indians.

3. That all legal business, documents, letters and actions can be on
25 common paper, with the requirement of the seal totally abolished.

Father Hidalgo appears below (the balding, white-haired man at the center) in a detail of a mural by the Mexican painter Diego Rivera (1886–1957).

---

## Discussing the Reading

1. How did the *Grito de Dolores* differ from Hidalgo's decree?

2. What was the purpose of Hidalgo's decree? What groups would have been in favor of the provisions of the decree and which would have been opposed?

3. How radical was Hidalgo? Justify your answer.

### CRITICAL THINKING
### Identifying Assumptions

Unlike Jefferson in his statute for religious freedom (see Reading 26B), Father Hidalgo did not indicate the philosophical assumptions that lay behind the provisions of his decree. For each of the three declarations, identify these assumptions.

---

# A Protest Against Machinery

# 28A

**TIME FRAME**

*Late 18th century*

**GEOGRAPHIC SETTING**

*England*

The Industrial Revolution was not seen by everyone as a means to a more productive and leisured society. Workers who were put out of work by machinery felt threatened, as this petition published in the newspapers of Leeds, England, on June 13, 1786, shows.

To the Merchants, Clothiers, and all such as wish well to the Staple Manufactory of this Nation.

The Humble address and petition of
5 thousands, who labor in the Cloth Manufactory.

RAWFOLDS MILL.

The Industrial Revolution created social unrest, which sometimes led to violence. Early in the 19th century, British workmen known as Luddites destroyed factory machinery in an attempt to preserve jobs. In 1812, a mob of 150 Luddites unsuccessfully attacked Rawfold's Mill (top left). At the bottom left is an illustration from a 19th-century novel depicting Luddite violence. The authorities dealt harshly with agitation by workers, as in the Peterloo Massacre in 1819 (right), when troops broke up a political rally at Manchester, killing eleven people and injuring hundreds.

Sheweth, That the Scribbling-Machines [used to prepare wool for spinning] have thrown thousands of
10 your petitioners out of employ, whereby they are brought into great distress, and are not able to procure a maintenance for their families and deprived them of the opportunity of
15 bringing up their children to labor. We have therefore to request, that prejudice and self-interest may be laid aside, and that you may pay that attention to the following facts, which the nature of the
20 case requires.

The number of Scribbling-Machines extending about seventeen miles southwest of Leeds exceed all belief, being no less than one hundred and seventy! and
25 as each machine will do as much in twelve hours, as ten men can in that time do by hand, (speaking within bounds) and they working night-and-day, one machine will do as much work
30 in one day as would otherwise employ twenty men. . . .

. . . Depopulation must be the consequence; trade being then lost, the landed interest will have no other satis-
35 faction but that of being last devoured.

We wish to propose a few queries to those who would plead for the further continuance of these machines:

Men of common sense must know,
40 that so many machines in use, take the work from the hands employed in Scribbling—and who did that business before machines were invented?

How are those men, thus thrown out
45 of employ to provide for their families—and what are they to put their children apprentice to, that the rising generation

may have something to keep them at work, in order that they may not be like vagabonds strolling about in idleness? Some say, Begin and learn some other business. Suppose we do; who will maintain our families, whilst we undertake the arduous task; and when we have learned it, how do we know we shall be any better for all our pains; for by the time we have served our second apprenticeship, another machine may arise, which may take away that business also; so that our families, being half pined [wasted away] whilst we are learning how to provide them with bread, will be wholly so during the period of our third apprenticeship.

But what are our children to do; are they to be brought up in idleness? Indeed as things are, it is no wonder to hear of so many executions; for our parts, though we may be thought illiterate men, our conceptions are, that bringing children up to industry, and keeping them employed, is the way to keep them from falling into those crimes, which an idle habit naturally leads to.

These things impartially considered will, we hope, be strong advocates in our favor; and we conceive that men of sense, religion, and humanity will be satisfied of the reasonableness, as well as necessity of this address, and that their own feelings will urge them to espouse the cause of us and our families.

Signed, in behalf of thousands, by
Joseph Hepworth
Robert Wood
Thomas Lobley
Thos. Blackburn

## Discussing the Reading

1. What are the consequences of more machinery as enumerated in the petition?
2. What did the petitioners say would happen if their children were "brought up in idleness"? Do you agree with their conclusions? Explain.

### CRITICAL THINKING
**Making Decisions**

What did the workers fear would happen if they trained for other jobs? To what extent does their fear apply to workers today? What solutions can you think of for the problem of retraining workers? What advantages would there be for the company that retrains its workers?

# How I Became a Socialist

# 28B

**TIME FRAME**

*Late 19th century*

**GEOGRAPHIC SETTING**

*Austria*

During the 19th century, issues such as the right to vote and poor working conditions drew huge numbers of women into politics. Some working-class women joined men's labor unions, others founded their own unions, while others sought to change society through socialist political activities. The following is the personal account of Anna Maier, a socialist worker in Austria in the 1890s.

When I am asked what brought me in touch with socialism, I must refer back to my childhood.... My father was a weaver, my mother a spooler, and other than that, they worked at whatever they could find. I am the youngest of twelve children and I learned very early what work is all about. When other children were out playing in the street, I would watch them with envy from the window until my mother would slap me to remind me that I had to work. . . . When one thinks that at six, a child has to give up all the pleasures of youth. That is a lot to ask! When I went to school my only desire was to learn. But that desire was an illusion because I had to get up at 5 o'clock, do some spooling, and then run off to school poorly dressed. After school I had to run home in order to do some more spooling before lunch. Then after school in the afternoons I had to spool again. I was able to accept that, but not being kept home from school to help with the work. But all the begging and crying in the world didn't help; I had to do what my mother said. When I was older and wiser, I often cursed all the splendors of nature because they had never meant anything to me.

When I turned thirteen my mother took me by the hand and we went to see the manager of a tobacco factory to get me a job. The manager refused to hire me but my mother begged him to change his mind, since she explained, my father had died. I was hired. When I was getting ready to go to work the next day, my mother told me that I was to keep quiet and do what I was told. That was easier said than done. The treatment you received in this factory was really brutal. Young girls were often abused or even beaten by the older women. I rebelled strongly against that. I tried anything that might help improve things for me. . . .

Several years went by. The *Women Workers' Newspaper* began to appear and a few issues were smuggled into the factory by one of the older women. The more I was warned to stay away from this woman, the more I went to her to ask her if she would lend me a copy of the newspaper since I didn't have enough money to buy my own. At that time work hours were very long and the pay was very low. When my friend lent me a copy of the newspaper, I had to keep it hidden and I couldn't even let my mother see it if I took it home. I came to understand many things, my circle of acquaintances grew and when a political organization was founded in Sternberg, the workers were urged to join— only the men, the women were left out. A party representative came to us since I was already married by then. When he came by for the third time I asked him if I wasn't mature enough to become a member of the organization. He was

Anna Maier's complaint about male domination of the German Social Democratic Party is reflected in this photograph of delegates to the party's Second Congress in 1871.

embarrassed but replied: "When do you want to?" So I joined and I am a member of the party to this day.

I attended all the meetings, took part in all the demonstrations, and it was not long before I was punished by the manager of the factory. I was taken off a good job and put in a poorer one just because I had become a Social Democrat. Nothing stopped me though; I said to myself, if this official is against it, out of fear to be sure, then it can't be all bad. . . . I have matured into a class-conscious fighter and I am now trying to win over mothers to the cause so that future children of the proletariat [prō′lə tar′ē ət; working class] will have a happier youth than I had.

## Discussing the Reading

1. What impact did education, or the lack of it, have on Anna Maier's life?

2. Why did Anna Maier join the Social Democratic party? What kinds of things did she hope might change for working women in the future?

### CRITICAL THINKING
### Analyzing Comparisons

Compare Anna Maier to the wife of the blacksmith in Reading 9A. What similarities are there in their roles as women? Would the blacksmith's wife have been interested in joining the Social Democratic party?

A *Punch* cartoon from 1850 satirizes Louis Napoleon's manipulation of the French constitution.

# Satirical Views of European Leaders

# 29A

**TIME FRAME**
*Mid-late 19th century*

**GEOGRAPHIC SETTING**
*Western Europe*

The art of political cartooning familiar from today's newspapers and magazines first appeared in England and France in the 18th century, growing out of an artistic tradition of caricature that had existed since the Renaissance. During the first half of the 19th century, as a free press grew along with the expansion of democracy in Europe, the art of the political cartoon developed as well. By the middle of the century there existed publications prominently featuring cartoons, notably the British comic magazine *Punch,* which first appeared in 1841. Above and on the next page are three cartoons showing prominent 19th-century European political leaders.

The earliest, a *Punch* cartoon from 1850, shows the French politician Louis Napoleon (1808–1873). A nephew of

emperor—as Napoleon III—in 1852 with dictatorial powers. The cartoon shows him first living in Constitution Hall, then taking off its roof, and finally upending and sitting on it. Napoleon III was forced into exile in 1871 after the Franco-Prussian War.

The second cartoon, from the German satirical weekly *Kladderadatsch* ("Mischief"), dates from 1883 and shows Otto von Bismarck (1815–1898). Bismarck, who was prime minister of Germany from 1862 to 1890, is best remembered for successful efforts to unify Germany and his domination of European diplomacy. Here he is pictured with a swollen stomach labeled "Unified Germany," and surrounded by possessions—like the pillow labeled "Morocco" under his foot—indicating the effects of his aggressive foreign policy.

The last cartoon, from an 1890 issue of *Punch,* shows the British politician William Ewart Gladstone (1809–1898). Liberal prime minister during much of the latter 19th century (1868–1874, 1880–1885, 1886, and 1892–1894), Gladstone was known to speak for long hours, haranguing voters, Parliament, and Cabinet over issues he thought needed attention.

19th-century political cartoons satirize Bismarck (above) and Gladstone (below).

Napoleon Bonaparte, he tried several times to become a leader in French politics. Finally, after the revolution of 1848, he was elected president by a large majority. But gradually he manipulated the French constitution until he was declared

## Discussing the Reading

1. Which of these three cartoons seems the most hostile toward its subject? Which seems the least hostile? Explain.

2. In what ways is a political cartoon more effective than an editorial? In what ways is it less effective?

### CRITICAL THINKING
### Making Decisions

In a democracy, should there be any limits on the way in which editorial writers and political cartoonists are allowed to present their views of public officials? Why or why not? (Remember that what is at issue here is opinion, not fact.)

# Treatment of Australian Aborigines

**TIME FRAME**
*Mid-19th century*

**GEOGRAPHIC SETTING**
*Australia*

From the very beginning of white settlement in Australia there was conflict with the native inhabitants, who were called aborigines [ab'ə rij'ə nēz], because settlers occupied lands that were aboriginal hunting grounds. While Australia changed from a penal colony to a self-governing democracy, the issue of aboriginal rights was rarely addressed. For example, aborigine testimony was not accepted in court and white settlers who murdered aborigines were rarely convicted by white juries. The following passage is an excerpt from a lecture given in 1865 by Gideon Lang, an Australian who wanted better treatment for the aborigines.

T he law in no way can or will punish [whites who murder aborigines]. The only remedy is to adopt the law of Victoria — admit the evidence of the
5 blacks. They are liars, no doubt, and have no idea of truth for truth's sake; but their evidence can be taken as it is here for what it is worth, like that of thieves and informers. When the blacks
10 understood that the whites were liable to be punished, communication would instantly be made to the Curator [official who dealt with aborigine affairs]; he would then examine the bodies; find if
15 the bullets corresponded with those of the accused whites; trace the horses of the party to their place of residence or halt; examine their horses' tracks at the place of murder, and compare it with
20 the horses' feet. He could thus get quite sufficient evidence in most cases to commit them, and, supported by the evidence of the blacks, enough to get them penal servitude, if not the gallows,
25 which many of them have well earned.

Large bodies of blacks are now collected near Rockhampton, and, feeling their strength, will never settle on any country quietly until they are fought
30 and beaten; but when that is done, it is sincerely to be hoped that some arrangement may be made for their having country assigned to them where they can live in safety. . . .

35 To conclude, the blacks have a tangible tribal government amongst themselves, and are sufficiently intelligent not only to make, but to enforce on the individual members of the tribe, any
40 reasonable arrangement that may be proposed by the whites for the joint occupation of the country for pasture and hunting; and it is the duty of the Queensland Government to introduce
45 and enforce some system that will at least give the blacks a chance of escaping summary extermination. . . .

As nearly two-thirds of the Australian continent is still to be occupied, and
50 that I believe the most numerously peopled by the blacks, it is a matter of grave importance, and a solemn duty for both the Government and the frontier squatters to adopt some system calculated to
55 diminish, if not altogether prevent, those fearful petty [frontier] wars, resulting in such destruction of property and life.

The causes are threefold:
60 *First.* That no Colonial Government has ever recognized any policy, authority, or property, tribal or personal, among the aborigines.

*Second.* They have been deprived of
65 their hunting grounds without any provision being made for them, the country having been occupied by the white settlers with as utter a disregard of their interests, rights, and even subsistence,
70 as if they had been wild dogs or kangaroos.

A peaceful encounter between a white settler and his aborigine neighbors is depicted in this 19th-century view of an Australian sheep station.

*Third.* From difficulties arising between the blacks and the pioneer squatters and their men. . . .

75 If only sheep stations [ranches] were in question the matter might more easily be managed, but the chief difficulty is with cattle, which are very often first put upon new country. The busi-
80 ness of the white man is to get his cattle to settle on the station—always a tedious, difficult operation. They are at first yarded and tailed like a flock of sheep, and then allowed to take up their
85 habitat on the different portions of the run, when they divide themselves into mobs, form their camps, and frequent particular water holes. But all this preliminary work is liable to be undone,
90 should any natives come upon the run, as the cattle detest the smell of them, and make off; and after being speared, they scatter in all directions, take to the scrubs, and become almost valueless.
95 The usual practice is, to prevent the blacks from coming on the run at all, so that they are not only cut off from their own water holes, but when the country is watered by one river or creek distant

100 from any other, they are deprived of water altogether for more than half the year; every drink is at the risk of their lives, until they are driven, . . . to perfect desperation.

105 As a large extent of country is taken up at one time, and this is done simultaneously on every station, they must go somewhere, a collision takes place, and the war begins. The blacks, thus driven
110 to sheer desperation, then kill far more white men than is generally imagined. I have known thirty-two killed, in one small district, in about two years, and little known beyond it. The blacks are
115 mercilessly shot down in turn, often without regard to age or sex, 156 blacks having been killed in the same district in the same time; and the blacks take revenge upon all, murdering even those
120 who are kindest to them, until the cruelties practiced on both sides are so atrocious as to be almost incredible.

## Discussing the Reading

1. Although the author wants better treatment for the aborigines, how does he reveal his own prejudice toward them?

2. For what reasons does the author think it is important to end conflict between the aborigines and the whites?

### CRITICAL THINKING
**Synthesizing Information**

Obvious parallels exist between the treatment of the aborigines by the Australians and the treatment of the Indians by the settlers in the American West. Imagine yourself testifying before a Congressional committee on Indian affairs sometime in the latter half of the 19th century. You have been asked to propose solutions to deal with the conflicts between Indians and whites. What do you propose?

# A Defense of Imperialism

**TIME FRAME**

*Late 19th century*

**GEOGRAPHIC SETTING**

*England*

Joseph Chamberlain (1836–1914) was a member of the British Parliament representing the working-class city of Birmingham. He was himself a wealthy manufacturer but advocated programs which he thought would benefit workers. He believed England's periodic depressions and unemployment could be avoided by incorporating into the British empire large foreign markets guaranteed for British goods. Thus he became one of the most outspoken advocates of British imperialism—especially in India and Africa, as he states in the following excerpt from one of his speeches.

We must look this matter in the face, and must recognize that in order that we may have more employment to give we must create more de-
5 mand. (Hear, hear.) Give me the demand for more goods and then I will undertake to give plenty of employment in making the goods; and the only thing, in my opinion, that the Government can
10 do in order to meet this great difficulty that we are considering, is so to arrange its policy that every inducement shall

With his sharp features and ribboned monocle, Joseph Chamberlain's face was a distinctive one. "No physiognomy," observed one biographer, "was better known to contemporaries, either at home or abroad."

be given to the demand; that new markets shall be created, and that old markets shall be effectually developed. (Cheers.) You are aware that some of my opponents please themselves occasionally by finding names for me— (laughter)—and among other names lately they have been calling me a Jingo [someone who favors an aggressive foreign policy]. (Laughter.) I am no more a Jingo than you are. (Hear, hear.) But for the reasons and arguments I have put before you tonight I am convinced that it is a necessity as well as a duty for us to uphold the dominion and empire which we now possess. (Loud cheers.) For these reasons, among others, I would never lose the hold which we now have over our great Indian dependency—(hear, hear)—by far the greatest and most valuable of all the customers we have or ever shall have in this country. For the same reasons I approve of the continued occupation of Egypt; and for the same reasons I have urged upon this Government, and upon previous Governments, the necessity for using every legitimate opportunity to extend our influence and control in that great African continent which is now being opened up to civilization and to commerce; and, lastly, it is for the same reasons that I hold that our navy should be strengthened—(loud cheers)—until its supremacy is so assured that we cannot be shaken in any of the possessions which we hold or may hold hereafter.

Believe me, if in any one of the places to which I have referred any change took place which deprived us of that control and influence of which I have been speaking, the first to suffer would be the workingmen of this country. Then, indeed, we should see a distress which would not be temporary, but which would be chronic, and we should find that England was entirely unable to support the enormous population which is now maintained by the aid of her foreign trade. If the workingmen of this country understand, as I believe they do—I am one of those who have had good reason through my life to rely upon their intelligence and shrewdness—if they understand their own interests, they will never lend any countenance to the doctrines of those politicians who never lose an opportunity of pouring contempt and abuse upon the brave Englishmen, who, even at this moment, in all parts of the world are carving out new dominions for Britain, and are opening up fresh markets for British commerce, and laying out fresh fields for British labor. (Applause.)

Titled "Mr. Joseph Chamberlain doing his best," this satirical view of Chamberlain as a flag-waving imperialist was done in 1901 by the famous British caricaturist Sir Max Beerbohm.

## Discussing the Reading

1. What were Chamberlain's reasons for supporting imperialism. (Look closely at lines 1–5 and 8–15.)

2. Why were India and Africa of special interest to Chamberlain?

### CRITICAL THINKING
### Making Hypotheses

Put yourself in the position of one of Chamberlain's political opponents. Develop arguments showing how his imperialistic policies could be harmful both to Britain and her colonies.

This street scene in Old Delhi was painted in 1907 by the British artist Walter Crane.

# First Doubts in My Imperialist Soul

30B

**TIME FRAME**
*Early 20th century*

**GEOGRAPHIC SETTING**
*Ceylon (Sri Lanka)*

Leonard Woolf (1880–1969) served as an administrator for the British imperial government in Ceylon (Sri Lanka today) from 1904 to 1911. As a result of his experiences there, he came to be a sensitive but vocal critic of the whole British imperial system. In the following excerpt from the second volume of his autobiography, Woolf described the episode that first prompted him to consider "whether I wanted to rule other people." The Tamils [tam′əlz] mentioned by Woolf are a people native to Sri Lanka.

M y unpopularity in [the town of] Jaffna was not undeserved. I meant well by the people of Jaffna, but, even when my meaning was well, and
5 also right — not always the case or the same thing — my methods were too ruthless, too much the "strong man." The difficulties and the friction made me for the first time dimly perceive the
10 problems of the imperialist. It is curious, looking back, to see how long it took me to become fully conscious of my position as a ruler of subject peoples. But I remember the moment when
15 for the first time I became fully aware of it and the awareness brought my first doubts whether I wanted to rule other people, to be an imperialist and a proconsul [a British colonial official]. . . .
20 In their [main] complaint the Jaffna Association [a citizens' group] pitched on something which in fact was not true. They said that one of their most respected members, Mr. Harry Sandera-
25 sekara, [sän′də rä sə kä′rä] a well-known lawyer, had been deliberately

121

hit in the face by the Office Assistant, Mr. Leonard Woolf. Mr. Sanderasekara had been driving in his trap, [a two-wheeled carriage] down the main street of Jaffna and [Mr. Woolf had been] riding up the street in the opposite direction. As they passed one another, Mr. Woolf turned his horse and deliberately hit Mr. Sanderasekara in the face with his riding whip.

When I first read this document, I was dismayed, because I could not understand how or why such an accusation could have been made against me. I knew and liked Sanderasekara. . . . Then suddenly I remembered vividly an incident which seemed to explain his misunderstanding and accusation. Shortly after [Hamlyn] Price took over as G. A. [Government Administrator], he and I were riding up the main street of the town, and when we got to the top of it. . . . I asked him to stop and look back down the street, for if he did so, he would see clearly how people had encroached upon the old line of the street by building verandahs. . . . out on to the highway. I remembered the long straight street in the glare and dust, the white houses and verandahs, and women's heads peering through blinds or round doors to see what the white men were stopping for. . . . And then I suddenly remembered that at some moment as my horse was dancing about, I had caught a glimpse out of the corner of my eye of a trap with Mr. Harry Sanderasekara sitting in it.

I gave my official explanation. . . . I said that I had never deliberately hit Mr. Sanderasekara or anyone else in Jaffna or anywhere else in the world with a riding whip. But I did remember how restive my horse had been as I pointed down the street with my whip, and I could only assume that, as the horse wheeled round, Mr. Sanderasekara was driving past and the whip, without my being aware of it, had passed near his face. . . . I doubted—and doubt—whether the Tamil Association and Mr. Sanderasekara believed or accepted it. It shocked me that these people should think that, as a white man and a ruler of Ceylon, I should consider the brown man, the Tamil, to be one of "the lesser breeds" and deliberately hit him in the face with my riding whip to show him that he must behave himself and keep in his place. For that is what all this meant. And perhaps for the first time I felt a twinge of doubt in my imperialist soul, a doubt whether we were not in the wrong, and the Jaffna Tamil Association and Mr. Sanderasekara in the right, not right in believing that I would, and had, hit him in the face, but right in feeling that my sitting on a horse arrogantly in the main street of their town was as good as a slap in the face.

## Discussing the Reading

1. If Leonard Woolf had been aware of Mr. Sanderasekara's impression at the time of the incident in the street, do you think that the two men could have discussed the episode and their differing points of view freely? Explain.

2. What was Woolf's attitude toward imperialism and his role as an administrator before the episode involving Mr. Sanderasekara? How did his attitude change as a result of this episode?

**CRITICAL THINKING**
**Analyzing Information**

Review Chamberlain's defense of imperialism in Reading 30A and compare his presentation of its economic advantages with Woolf's insight into the moral dilemmas it creates. How might each man react to the other's account of imperialism?

# "We'll Be Home at Christmas"

**TIME FRAME**
*Early 20th century*

**GEOGRAPHIC SETTING**
*Austria*

When World War I began in August, 1914, statesmen as well as ordinary people were actually joyful and excited. Europe had not endured a long war for over fifty years. Many memoirs of the time record that it had been one of the most beautiful summers Europe had ever seen—cool, pleasant, sunny, and green. Now everyone thought there would be a few glorious battles, with medals and honor to be attained, and the war would be over. In England and France as well as Germany and Austria young men all said they would be home by Christmas. But instead of the brief, exhilarating adventure they had anticipated, these young men encountered the horror of a war that dragged on for years of murderous stalemate, with millions killed and maimed, and no glory in the mud and trenches. Stefan Zweig, [zwīg] (1881–1942) an Austrian poet, knew this when he wrote his autobiography in 1941, but he still recalled in the following excerpt the excitement of the moment in Vienna, in the summer of 1914.

Exuberant civilians escort German soldiers mobilized at the beginning of World War I in the photograph above. In the drawing at the left, army officers relax in a pre-war Viennese cafe.

123

The next morning I was in Austria. In every station placards had been put up announcing general mobilization. The trains were filled with fresh recruits, banners were flying, music sounded, and in Vienna I found the entire city in a tumult . . . . There were parades in the street, flags, ribbons, and music burst forth everywhere, young recruits were marching triumphantly, their faces lighting up at the cheering— they, the John Does and Richard Roes who usually go unnoticed and uncelebrated.

And to be truthful, I must acknowledge that there was a majestic, rapturous, and even seductive something in this first outbreak of the people from which one could escape only with difficulty. And in spite of all my hatred and aversion for war, I should not like to have missed the memory of those first days. As never before, thousands and hundreds of thousands felt what they should have felt in peacetime, that they belonged together. A city of two million, a country of nearly fifty million, in that hour felt that they were participating in world history, in a moment which would never recur, and that each one was called upon to cast his infinitesimal self into the glowing mass, there to be purified of all selfishness. All differences of class, rank, and language were flooded over at that moment by the rushing feeling of fraternity. Strangers spoke to one another in the streets, people who had avoided each other for years shook hands, everywhere one saw excited faces. Each individual experienced an exaltation of his ego, he was no longer the isolated person of former times, he had been incorporated into the mass, he was part of the people, and his person, his hitherto unnoticed person, had been given meaning. The petty mailclerk, who ordinarily sorted letters early and late, who sorted constantly, who sorted from Monday until Saturday without interruption; the clerk, the cobbler, had suddenly achieved a romantic possibility in life: he could become a hero, and everyone who wore a uniform was already being cheered by the women, and greeted beforehand with this romantic appellation by those who had to remain behind. They acknowledged the unknown power which had lifted them out of their everyday existence.

. . . What did the great mass know of war in 1914, after nearly half a century of peace? They did not know war, they had hardly given it a thought. It had become legendary, and distance had made it seem romantic and heroic. They still saw it in the perspective of their school readers and of paintings in museums; brilliant cavalry attacks in glittering uniforms, the fatal shot always straight through the heart, the entire campaign a resounding march of victory—"We'll be home at Christmas," the recruits shouted laughingly to their mothers in August of 1914.

## Discussing the Reading

1. In Stefan Zweig's view, what made the atmosphere of August, 1914, so special?

2. Can individuals experience the same types of feelings through involvement with peacetime activities that Zweig associates with the outbreak of war?

**CRITICAL THINKING**
**Making Hypotheses**

Using Zweig's depiction of Austria in 1914 as a basis, develop a hypothesis to account for the initial popularity of World War I.

# World War I—Enter and Exit

*Early 20th century*

*England*

The product of a comfortable middle-class background, Vera Brittain (1893–1970) broke away from her sheltered family life to serve four trying years during World War I as a Red Cross nurse in army hospitals in London, Malta, and France. For almost ten years after the war, Brittain struggled to find the appropriate medium through which to convey the war's impact on her own life and the lives of the men and women of her generation. She first contemplated writing a novel, then reproducing the diary she had kept from 1913 to 1918, using fictitious names for the people mentioned. Finally she resolved that the truth of the experience could only be revealed by setting her personal story against the larger background of war and social change. The subtitle of her book *Testament of Youth*—"An Autobiographical Study of the Years 1900–1925"—emphasizes her intent to present history through an account of her personal life. The following excerpts from *Testament of Youth* deal with the opening days of World War I in August, 1914, and with its final day, Armistice Day, November 11, 1918. In between she had lost many of the people closest to her, including her brother Edward and her fiancé, Roland Leighton.

The impact of World War I is reflected in the changed appearance of Vera Brittain, shown in a prewar photograph above and in her nurse's uniform at the right.

## 1914

When the Great War broke out, it came to me not as a superlative tragedy, but as an interruption of the most exasperating kind to my personal plans. . . .

My diary for August 3rd, 1914, contains a most incongruous mixture of war and tennis.

The day was Bank Holiday [a weekday on which British banks are closed], and a tennis tournament had been arranged at the Buxton Club. I had promised to play with my discouraged but still faithful suitor, and did not in the least want to forgo the amusement that I knew this partnership would afford me—particularly as the events reported in the newspapers seemed too incredible to be taken quite seriously.

"I do not know," I wrote in my diary, "how we all managed to play tennis so calmly and take quite an interest in the result. I suppose it is because we all know so little of the real meaning of war 25 that we are so indifferent. B. and I had to owe 30. It was good handicapping as we had a very close game with everybody." . . .

After that [August 4] events moved, 30 even in Buxton, very quickly. The German cousins of some local acquaintances left the town in a panic. My parents rushed over in the car to familiar shops in Macclesfield and Leek, where 35 they laid in stores of cheese, bacon, and butter under the generally shared impression that by next week we might all be besieged by the Germans. Wild rumors circulated from mouth to 40 mouth; they were more plentiful than the newspapers, over which a free fight broke out on the station platform every time a batch came by train from London or Manchester. Our elderly cook, who 45 had three Reservist sons, dissolved into continuous tears and was too much upset to prepare the meals with her usual competence; her young daughter-in-law, who had had a baby only the 50 previous Friday, became hysterical and had to be forcibly restrained from getting up and following her husband to the station. One or two Buxton girls were hurriedly married to officers sum-55 moned to unknown destinations. Pandemonium swept over the town. Holiday trippers wrestled with one another for the *Daily Mail;* habitually quiet and respectable citizens struggled like 60 wolves for the provisions in the foodshops, and vented upon the distracted assistants their dismay at learning that all prices had suddenly gone up.

## 1918

When the sound of victorious guns burst over London at 11 a.m. on November 11th, 1918, the men and women who looked incredulously into 5 each other's faces did not cry jubilantly: "We've won the War!" They only said: "The War is over."

From Millbank I heard the maroons [fireworks that simulate the sound of 10 cannons] crash with terrifying clearness, and, like a sleeper who is determined to go on dreaming after being told to wake up, I went on automatically washing the dressing bowls in the an-15 nex outside my hut. . . .

And as I dried the bowls I thought: "It's come too late for me. Somehow I knew, even at Oxford, that it would. Why couldn't it have ended rationally, 20 as it might have ended, in 1916, instead of all that trumpet-blowing against a negotiated peace, and the ferocious talk of secure civilians about marching to Berlin? It's come five months too late—or is 25 it three years? It might have ended last June, and let Edward, at least, be saved! Only five months—it's such a little time, when Roland died nearly three years ago." . . .

30 Late that evening, when supper was over, a group of elated V.A.D.s [Army nurses] who were anxious to walk through Westminster and Whitehall to Buckingham Palace prevailed upon me 35 to join them. Outside the Admiralty a crazy group of convalescent Tommies [British soldiers] were collecting specimens of different uniforms and bundling their wearers into flagstrewn 40 taxis; with a shout they seized two of my companions and disappeared into the clamorous crowd, waving flags and shaking rattles. Wherever we went a burst of enthusiastic cheering greeted 45 our Red Cross uniform, and complete strangers adorned with wound stripes rushed up and shook me warmly by the hand. After the long, long blackness, it seemed like a fairy-tale to see the street 50 lamps shining through the chill November gloom.

I detached myself from the others and

walked slowly up Whitehall, with my heart sinking in a sudden cold dismay. Already this was a different world from the one that I had known during four life-long years, a world in which people would be light-hearted and forgetful, in which themselves and their careers and their amusements would blot out political ideals and great national issues. And in that brightly lit, alien world I should have no part. All those with whom I had really been intimate were gone; not one remained to share with me the heights and the depths of my memories. As the years went by and youth departed and remembrance grew dim, a deeper and ever deeper darkness would cover the young men who were once my contemporaries.

For the time I realized, with all that full realization meant, how completely everything that had hitherto made up my life had vanished with Edward and Roland, with Victor and Geoffrey. The War was over; a new age was beginning; but the dead were dead and would never return.

## Discussing the Reading

1. Review Reading 31A. How are Stefan Zweig's and Vera Brittain's accounts similar? How are they different?

2. What is the mood of the second excerpt? How did the war change Vera Brittain?

### CRITICAL THINKING
### Analyzing Information

Using these excerpts from *Testament of Youth* as evidence, analyze the changes in British public opinion toward the war.

# The Cause of Bloody Sunday

# 32A

**TIME FRAME**
*Early 20th century*

**GEOGRAPHIC SETTING**
*Russia*

In January, 1905, strikes and unanswered demands for political reform spurred thousands of Russian workers to march to the Winter Palace in St. Petersburg where Tsar Nicholas II (1868–1918) was supposed to be in residence, to present him with the petition below. Hundreds of the unarmed demonstrators were killed when troops fired on the crowd. The day came to be known as Bloody Sunday.

Attacking the brutality of the tsarist government, this cartoon by John T. McCutcheon (1870–1949) of the *Chicago Tribune* appeared after Bloody Sunday.

Struck by a volley of shots fired by troops lined up before the Winter Palace, dead and wounded workers are depicted in a painting by I. Vladimirov (1870–1947).

S ire! We, the workers and residents of the city of St. Petersburg, of various ranks and stations, our wives, children, and helpless old people, our
5 parents, have come to you, Sire, to seek justice and protection. We have become destitute, we are being persecuted, we are overburdened with work, we are being insulted, we are not regarded as
10 human beings, we are treated as slaves who must endure their bitter fate in silence. We have suffered, but even so we are being pushed more and more into the pool of poverty, disfranchise-
15 ment, and ignorance. We are being stifled by despotism and arbitrary rule, and we are gasping for breath. We have no strength left, Sire. We have reached the limit of endurance. For us that ter-
20 rible moment has arrived, when death is preferable to the continuance of unbearable torture. . . .

We have been enslaved, and enslaved under the auspices of your officials,
25 with their aid, and with their cooperation. Every one of us who has the temerity to raise his voice in defense of the interests of the working class and the people is thrown into jail and sent
30 into exile. We are punished for a good heart and for a sympathetic soul as we would be for a crime. . . .

Sire! Is this in accordance with God's laws, by the grace of which you reign? Is
35 it possible to live under such laws? Isn't it better to die—for all of us, the toiling people of all Russia, to die? . . . This is the dilemma before us, Sire, and this is why we have assembled before the
40 walls of your palace. This is our last resort. Don't refuse to help your people, lead them out of the grave of disfranchisement, poverty, and ignorance, give them an opportunity to determine their
45 own fate, and cast off the unbearable yoke of the bureaucrats. Tear down the wall between you and your people, and let them rule the country with you. . . .

Look without anger, attentively, at our
50 requests; they are not intended for an
evil, but for a good cause, for both of us,
Sire. We do not talk arrogantly, but from
a realization of the necessity to extricate
ourselves from a plight unbearable to all
55 of us. Russia is too vast, her needs too
diverse and numerous to be run only by
bureaucrats. It is necessary to have popular representation; it is necessary that
the people help themselves and govern
60 themselves. Only they know their real
needs. Do not reject their help; take it;
command at once, forthwith, that there
be summoned the representatives of the
land of Russia from all classes, all strata,
65 including also the representatives of the
workers. Let there be a capitalist, a
worker, a bureaucrat, a priest, a doctor,
and a teacher—let them all, whoever
they are, elect their own representa-
70 tives. Let everyone be equal and free in
the matter of suffrage, and for that purpose command that the elections for the
Constituent Assembly be carried out on
the basis of universal, secret, and equal
75 suffrage. . . .

And if you do not so decree, and do
not respond to our supplication, we will
die here, in this square, in front of your
palace. We have nowhere else to go and
80 it is useless to go. There are only two
roads open to us: one toward freedom
and happiness, the other toward the
grave. Let our lives be the sacrifice for
suffering Russia. We do not regret this
85 sacrifice. We are glad to make it.

## Discussing the Reading

1. How do the petitioners perceive the tsar?
2. Review Reading 12A. Why were the English barons successful in dealing with King John while the Russian workers were not in dealing with the tsar?

**CRITICAL THINKING**
**Assessing Cause and Effect**

Under what circumstances can nonviolent protests work?

# Stalin's Forced Collectivization

# 32B

**TIME FRAME**
*Early 1930s*

**GEOGRAPHIC SETTING**
*Soviet Union*

Between 1929 and 1933 Soviet dictator Joseph Stalin (1879–1953) undertook a policy whose goal was to eliminate pri-vate ownership of farms. All Soviet agri-culture was to be conducted by the state on great "collectivized" farms which were owned and administered by the govern-ment. Stalin argued that these state farms would be more efficient, though Soviet agriculture has yet to be as productive as the West's private agricultural system. Of course, successful individual farmers called kulaks [kü läks'] resisted Stalin's plan, and even poor peasants barely making a living were not eager to be forced onto state farms. Stalin, however, treated this resistance as he did all other difficulties—with force, intimidation, and

brutality. As many as 5 million kulaks and peasants were killed or sent to forced labor camps in the early 1930s. The fol-lowing is an excerpt from an unpublished novel by a Russian who participated in the collectivization—or "dekulakization"—campaign and later revealed the human tragedy that resulted from Stalin's policy.

The door opened and the brigade burst into the house. The OGPU [secret police] officer in charge of the operation was in front, holding a
5 revolver.

"Hands up!"

Morgunov [môr gü′nôf; the officer in charge] was barely able to distinguish the frail figure of the class enemy. He was barefoot, wearing white drawers and a dark undershirt; a dishevelled beard stuck out on a face that was long unshaven. His eyes, wide with terror, darted from place to place. The lined face flinched, the coarse brown hands were trembling. . . .

Gusts of freezing air came through the open door into the well-heated little hut. Members of the dekulakization brigade were already standing at each window, their faces stern. Expecting something dreadful to happen, they all were ready to rush into battle for their cause, for soviet power, for socialism. But the kulak-agent Terentyev [tėr ent′yef] never thought of resisting. He kept blinking and crossing himself, shifting from one foot to the other, as though he were standing on something hot, and suddenly he began to sob, his whole body shaken by convulsive gasps. He was bending over in a peculiar position, shuddering, and small, glistening tears, one after another, rolled down the coarsened, weather-beaten face. His wife, no longer young, jumped down from the high sleeping bench and began to wail at the top of her voice; the children started to cry; and a calf, apparently rather sick and lying beside the stove, added to the clamor. Morgunov looked around, quite horrified. He saw that the hut contained only the one room and the large Russian stove. In the front corner beneath the icons were two simple wooden benches and a crude table put together from planks. There was no sign of a dresser, or a bed, or a chair. On the shelves there were some wooden bowls, worn by years of use, and some old wooden spoons. Some oven forks and buckets of water stood by the stove, and on the left against the wall, a large old-fashioned trunk.

The class enemy!

The poster below was created by the Soviet government to convince peasants of the advantages of the collective farms. In the upper panels, three peasants can individually accomplish little. In the lower panels, the three succeed by joining together on a collective.

The representatives of authority had already informed Terentyev that he was under arrest. He was to be dekulakized
60 and deported straight away. All his possessions would be confiscated. His family would follow shortly, but their destination was not known. He could take with him only the clothes on his
65 back and a change of underwear.

Terentyev trembled and wept. "How can you call us kulaks? What for? What have I done?" He got no reply. Roughly breaking the locks, they opened the
70 trunk and the food cupboard and pulled out some sort of footgear, sackcloth, and foodstuffs.

"What for? What have I done?"

"Nothing. You're a kulak, a kulak-
75 agent. You're against the collective farm. You don't want to join and you're upsetting everything. And that's all there is to it!" And they started making a list of all his goods and possessions.

## Discussing the Reading

1. Is Terentyev a "successful individual farmer"? Why or why not?

2. The fifth amendment to the U.S. Constitution states that "no person shall be . . . deprived of life, liberty, or property, without due process of law; nor shall private property be taken for public use, without just compensation." In what ways would such a provision have been helpful to Terentyev?

**CRITICAL THINKING**
**Recognizing Values**

"If it is the responsibility of the government to address the wrongs listed in Reading 32A (poverty, disfranchisement, and ignorance), then it is also the responsibility of the government to introduce reforms to improve the economy." Agree or disagree with this statement. When are the rights of society more important than the rights of individuals?

# A National Home for the Jewish People

# 33A

**TIME FRAME**
*Early 20th century*

**GEOGRAPHIC SETTING**
*England*

Jewish aspirations to create a national home grew rapidly after 1900. Many Jews felt that only with the legal and military protection of their own nation-state would they be safe from the routine discrimination and periodic persecution that had been their experience as exiles. The most militant of these Jews, known as Zionists, wanted to build a state in their original homeland, Palestine, at that time a part of the Turkish Empire. During World War I the Turks lost their possessions in the Middle East to Britain and France. Palestine ultimately became a British mandate

(a territory or colony given to a nation to govern). The British government—strongly influenced by its Foreign Secretary Arthur James Balfour [bal'fur] (1848–1930), who was sympathetic to the Zionists—became convinced that its support of the Zionist program would not only be a humanitarian gesture but would also serve British imperial interests in the Middle East. In 1917 Balfour wrote a letter to a prominent British Zionist, Lord Rothschild, about postwar British policies for Palestine. This letter, the Balfour Declaration, appears on the next page.

One of the milestones in the path that led to the modern state of Israel, the Balfour Declaration also expressed concern for the rights of Arab Palestinians.

Foreign Office,
November 2nd, 1917

Dear Lord Rothschild,

I have much pleasure in conveying to you, on behalf of His Majesty's Government, the following declaration of sympathy with Jewish Zionist aspirations which has been submitted to, and approved by, the Cabinet.

"His Majesty's Government view with favour the establishment in Palestine of a national home for the Jewish people, and will use their best endeavours to facilitate the achievement of this object, it being clearly understood that nothing shall be done which may prejudice the civil and religious rights of existing non-Jewish communities in Palestine, or the rights and political status enjoyed by Jews in any other country"

I should be grateful if you would bring this declaration to the knowledge of the Zionist Federation.

## Discussing the Reading

1. What did the British government promise the Zionists in the Balfour Declaration?

2. What did the British do to protect the rights of Arabs in Palestine?

3. The Balfour Declaration is considered a very controversial document. In what way might it be said that the British tried to please everyone and pleased no one? Why do you think the British felt they could make the promises given in the Balfour Declaration?

### CRITICAL THINKING
### Synthesizing Information

In what ways is the situation of the Palestinians in Israel today similar to that of Zionists in 1917? In what ways is it different?

# Hitler's Charisma

# 33B

**TIME FRAME**
*Mid-1930s*

**GEOGRAPHIC SETTING**
*Germany*

One of the characteristics of the rise to power of German dictator Adolf Hitler (1889–1945) was the way he could thrill and excite crowds with his speeches. It is difficult for non-German speakers to understand what intrigued crowds so much, for in newsreels of Hitler speaking he appears merely loud and frantic and certainly not persuasive. Nevertheless, even as described below by a journalist unsympathetic to the Nazis, a German woman named Lilo Linke, Hitler's message clearly addressed deeply felt emotional concerns of Germans: they had been humiliated by World War I, unjustly treated by world opinion, and Hitler promised they would once again stand tall and proud on the stage of history.

A t this moment the whole audience rose from their seats, most of them with wild cheers—from the back,
behind an S.A. [Nazi stormtrooper]
5 man who carried a large swastika flag, and a drumming and blowing and dinning band, a procession of S.A. men and Hitler Youth marched towards the platform. I enjoyed the right to remain
10 seated as a member of the press. When they were half-way through the hall, the curtain draped behind the platform opened and Hitler, wearing a dark suit, stepped forward to the decorated desk.
15 The audience howled with enthusiastic madness, lifting their right arms in the Fascist salute.

Hitler stood unmoved. At last, when the crowd was already hoarse with
20 shouting, he made a commanding gesture to silence them, and slowly obeying, they grew calmer, as a dog, called to order by its master after wild play, lies down, exhaustedly snarling.

132

For an hour and a half Hitler spoke, every few minutes interrupted by fanatic acclamations which grew into a frenzy after such phrases as:

"Today the world treats us like outcasts. But they will respect us again when we show them our good old German sword, flashing high above our heads!"

Or: "Pacifism is the contemptible religion of the weak; a real man is not afraid of defending his rights by force."

Or: "Those foreign blood-suckers, those degenerate asphalt-democrats, those cunning Jews, those whining pacifists, those corrupted November criminals [men who had agreed to the German surrender and armistice of November 1918]—we'll knock them all down with our fists without pardoning a single one of them."

He thrust his chin forward. His voice, hammering the phrases with an obsessed energy, became husky and shrill and began to squeak more and more frequently. His whole face was covered with sweat; a greasy tress kept on falling on his forehead, however often he pushed it back.

Speaking with a stern face, he crossed his arms over his breast—the imposing attitude of one who stood under his own

Adolf Hitler appears as the knightly hero of a medieval romance in "The Flag Bearer," a painting done by a German artist during the 1930s. The photograph below shows young Germans saluting at a Nazi youth rally in May, 1933.

supreme control. But a moment later a force bursting out of him flung them into the air, where they implored,
60 threatened, accused, condemned, assisted by his hands and fists. Later, exhausted, he crossed them on his back and began to march a few steps to and fro along the front of the platform, a lion
65 behind the bars of his cage, waiting for the moment when the door will be opened to jump on the terror-stricken enemy.

The audience was breathlessly under
70 his spell. This man expressed their thoughts, their feelings, their hopes; a new prophet had arisen—many saw in him already another Christ, who predicted the end of their sufferings and
75 had the power to lead them into the promised land if they were only prepared to follow him.

Every word he said was true. They had won the war—yes. Been deprived
80 of the reward for their heroism by a number of traitors—yes. Had suffered incessantly ever since—yes. Been enslaved, suppressed, exploited—yes, yes, yes. But the day had arrived when
85 they would free and revenge themselves—yes.

A single question as to reason or proof or possibility would have shat-tered the whole argument, but nobody
90 asked it—the majority because they had begun to think with their blood, which condemns all logic, and the others because they sat amazed, despairing, and hopeless in a small boat tossed
95 about by the foaming waves of emotional uproar which surrounded it.

---

## Discussing the Reading

1. How did the staging of this event encourage the desired response of the audience?

2. Analyze Hitler's quotes in lines 29–45. Paraphrase each, omitting the emotional terms. Characterize the material that remains. How interested was Hitler in appealing to rationality and logic?

3. Review Machiavelli's definition of prestige in Reading 12B. Is charisma an essential part of the prestige of a 20th-century leader? Is it possible to be a successful leader without charisma?

**CRITICAL THINKING**
**Evaluating Sources of Information**

What is the author's view of Hitler? Cite sentences that indicate her feelings about him.

---

# Munich: A Defeat Without a War

# 34A

**TIME FRAME**
*Late 1930s*

**GEOGRAPHIC SETTING**
*England*

When the prime minister of Great Britain, Neville Chamberlain, returned from his September 29, 1938, meeting with Hitler in Munich, he brought back an agreement between Great Britain and Germany that the two nations would never go to war, provided Germany did not take any more territory in Europe by force. Chamberlain claimed that he had achieved "peace with honor." The British public was relieved, for war with Germany had appeared imminent. People cheered and demonstrated their support in the streets. Winston Churchill, a member of Parliament, took the unpopular stand of opposing the Munich agreement and, in the speech that follows, warned that Hitler would not abide by the peace.

---

W hen I think of the fair hopes of a long peace which still lay before

We, the German Führer and Chancellor and the British Prime Minister, have had a further meeting today and are agreed in recognising that the question of Anglo-German relations is of the first importance for the two countries and for Europe.

We regard the agreement signed last night and the Anglo-German Naval Agreement as symbolic of the desire of our two peoples never to go to war with one another again.

We are resolved that the method of consultation shall be the method adopted to deal with any other questions that may concern our two countries, and we are determined to continue our efforts to remove possible sources of difference and thus to contribute to assure the peace of Europe.

*September 30, 1938*

Waving the document containing the Munich Agreement, British Prime Minister Neville Chamberlain is shown returning to England on September 30, 1938. The document itself appears on the right.

Europe at the beginning of 1933 when Herr Hitler first obtained power, and of
5 all the opportunities of arresting the growth of the Nazi power which have been thrown away, when I think of the immense combinations and resources which have been neglected or squan-
10 dered, I cannot believe that a parallel exists in the whole course of history. . . .

We are in the presence of a disaster of the first magnitude which has befallen Great Britain and France. Do not let us
15 blind ourselves to that. It must now be accepted that all the countries of Central and Eastern Europe will make the best terms they can with the triumphant Nazi Power. . . .
20 The Prime Minister desires to see cordial relations between this country and Germany. There is no difficulty at all in having cordial relations with the German people. Our hearts go out to
25 them. But they have no power. You must have diplomatic and correct relations, but there can never be friendship between the British democracy and the Nazi Power, that Power which spurns
30 Christian ethics, which cheers its onward course by a barbarous paganism, which vaunts the spirit of aggression and conquest, which derives strength and perverted pleasure from
35 persecution, and uses, as we have seen, with pitiless brutality the threat of murderous force. That Power cannot ever be the trusted friend of the British democracy. . . .
40 I have been casting about to see how measures can be taken to protect us from this advance of the Nazi Power,

and to secure those forms of life which are so dear to us. What is the sole method that is open? . . . An effort at rearmament the like of which has not been seen ought to be made forthwith, and all the resources of this country and all its united strength should be bent to that task. . . .

I do not grudge our loyal, brave people, who were ready to do their duty no matter what the cost, who never flinched under the strain of last week—I do not grudge them the natural, spontaneous outburst of joy and relief when they learned that the hard ordeal would no longer be required of them at the moment; but they should know the truth. They should know that there has been gross neglect and deficiency in our defenses; they should know that we have sustained a defeat without a war, the consequences of which will travel far with us along our road; they should know that we have passed an awful milestone in our history, when the whole equilibrium of Europe has been deranged, and that the terrible words have for the time being been pronounced against the Western democracies:

"Thou are weighed in the balance and found wanting."

And do not suppose that this is the end. This is only the beginning of the reckoning. This is only the first sip, the first foretaste of a bitter cup which will be proffered to us year by year unless by a supreme recovery of moral health and martial vigor, we arise again and take our stand for freedom as in the olden time.

## Discussing the Reading

1. What were Churchill's objections to Britain's foreign policy during the 1930s? What course would he have followed? Based on Churchill's description of Britain during this period, what else could Chamberlain have done in 1938 besides negotiate?

2. Reread "1914" in Reading 31B. Compare British feelings about war in 1914 with the way they are characterized by Churchill in lines 51–59. How had experience changed attitudes toward war in Europe?

### CRITICAL THINKING
### Making Generalizations

How can the advice Churchill gave to the British be applied to our own government's foreign policy today?

# Truman's Decision to Drop the Bomb

# 34B

**TIME FRAME**
*Mid-1940s*

**GEOGRAPHIC SETTING**
*United States*

When Vice-President Harry Truman became President in April, 1945, upon the death of Franklin Roosevelt, he claimed that the research on the atomic bomb had been kept so secret that even he knew nothing of the existence of this frightening weapon. Yet within a few months he had to make the momentous decision whether or not to use the bomb on Japan. In the following excerpts from his memoirs he gives his reasons for his

decision to use the atomic bomb, thus opening the world to a future of possible nuclear war.

T he historic message of the first [test] explosion of an atomic bomb was flashed to me in a message from Secretary of War Stimson on the morning of July 16. The most secret and the most daring enterprise of the war had succeeded. We were now in possession of a weapon that would not only revolutionize war but could alter the course of history and civilization . . . .

We knew that the bomb would receive its first test in mid-July. If the test of the bomb was successful, I wanted to afford Japan a clear chance to end the fighting before we made use of this newly gained power. If the test should fail, then it would be even more important to us to bring about a surrender before we had to make a physical conquest of Japan. General Marshall told me that it might cost half a million American lives to force the enemy's surrender on his home grounds. But the test was now successful . . . .

. . . I had then set up a committee of top men and had asked them to study with great care the implications the new weapon might have for us. It was their recommendation that the bomb be used against the enemy as soon as it could be done. They recommended further that it should be used without specific warning and against a target that would clearly show its devastating strength. I had realized, of course, that an atomic bomb explosion would inflict damage and casualties beyond imagination. On the other hand, the scientific advisers of the committee reported, "We can propose no technical demonstration likely to bring an end to the war; we see no acceptable alternative to direct military use." It was their conclusion that no technical demonstration they might propose, such as over a deserted island, would be likely to bring the war to an end. It had to be used against an enemy target.

The final decision of where and when to use the atomic bomb was up to me. Let there be no mistake about it. I

A few hours after the first atomic bomb was detonated over the Japanese city of Hiroshima, on August 6, 1945, victims of the blast are shown waiting to receive first aid.

regarded the bomb as a military weapon and never had any doubt that it should be used . . . .

In deciding to use this bomb I wanted to make sure that it would be used as a weapon of war in the manner prescribed by the laws of war. That meant that I wanted it dropped on a military target. I had told Stimson that the bomb should be dropped as nearly as possibly upon a war production center of prime military importance.

Stimson's staff had prepared a list of cities in Japan that might serve as targets. Kyoto, though favored by General Arnold as a center of military activity, was eliminated when Secretary Stimson pointed out that it was a cultural and religious shrine of the Japanese. Four cities were finally recommended as targets: Hiroshima, Kokura, Niigata, and Nagasaki. . . .

Nagasaki. . . .

On August 6, the fourth day of the journey home from Potsdam, came the historic news that shook the world. I was eating lunch with members of the *Augusta's* crew when Captain Frank Graham, White House Map Room watch officer, handed me the . . . message: Following message regarding Manhattan received. "Hiroshima bombed visually with only one tenth cover at 052315A. There was no fighter opposition and no flak. Parsons reports 15 minutes after drop as follows: 'Results clear cut successful in all respects. Visible effects greater than in

Recording the beginning of the nuclear age, this watch was found in the ruins of Hiroshima.

any test. Conditions normal in airplane following delivery.' "

I was greatly moved. I telephoned Byrnes aboard ship to give him the news and then said to the group of sailors around me, "This is the greatest thing in history. It's time for us to get home."

---

## Discussing the Reading

1. What did President Truman mean when he said, "This is the greatest thing in history"? On what assumptions did he base his remark? Do you agree with him?

2. What did Truman recognize would be the consequences of his decision to use the atomic bomb? Did he have adequate information to make his decision? What consequences did he not foresee?

**CRITICAL THINKING**
**Making Decisions**

What circumstances, if any, are there that would warrant the use of modern nuclear weapons?

---

# This is Hungary Calling!

**TIME FRAME**
*Mid-1950s*

**GEOGRAPHIC SETTING**
*Hungary*

In October, 1956, Hungarians overthrew their pro-Soviet government in an armed rebellion. The Soviet Union responded by invading Hungary, killing rebellious Hungarian citizens, and installing another pro-Soviet Hungarian government. Troops entered Budapest, the capital, on November 4, and by that evening the rebellion had been crushed. Throughout that day Hungarian radio stations in the control of the resisters broadcast appeals for help to the United Nations and the West. None came.

---

[*Free Radio Dunapentele, 8:30* A.M.] This is the Free Radio of the Dunapentele National Committee on 36 short-wave meter band. The treacherous occupation forces attacked Budapest and several other cities in the country! The battle is on. . . . Hungarian[s] are fighting as one man against the intruders and will keep on fighting for the sacred cause of Hungarian Revolution to their last drop of blood! The situation of our nation is tragic but not hopeless. . . .

[*Free Radio Rakoczi* (rä kô′shē), *1:55* P.M.] This is Hungary calling! This is Hungary calling! The last free station. Forward to the United Nations. Early this morning Soviet troops launched a general attack on Hungary. We are requesting you to send us immediate aid in the form of parachute troops over the Transdanubian provinces. It is possible that our broadcasts will soon come to the same fate as the other Hungarian broadcasting stations. . . . For the sake of God and freedom, help Hungary!

[*Free Radio Petofi* (pet′ô fē), *2:34* P.M.] Civilized people of the world, listen and come to our aid. Not with declarations, but with force, with soldiers, with arms. Do not forget that there is no stopping the wild onslaught of Bolshevism. Your turn will also come, if we perish. Save our souls! Save our souls! . . . Civilized peoples of the world! We implore you in the name of justice, freedom, and

TWENTY CENTS

JANUARY 7, 1957

MAN OF THE YEAR

# TIME

## THE WEEKLY NEWSMAGAZINE

HUNGARIAN
FREEDOM FIGHTER

Celebrating the heroic determination of the young people involved in the revolt in Hungary in October, 1956, *Time* magazine's annual "Man of the Year" award was given to the "Hungarian Freedom Fighter." The photograph on the right shows a street battle in Budapest.

the binding moral principle of active solidarity to help us. Our ship is sinking. Light is failing. The shadows grow
40 darker every hour over the soil of Hungary. Listen to our cry, civilized peoples of the world, and act. Extend us your fraternal aid. SOS! SOS! May God be with you!

45 [*Moscow's response, Radio Moscow, 3:10* P.M.] . . . Many Hungarian workers who were deceived by the insurgents' propaganda have had their eyes opened. They have seen how the ene-
50 mies of the people's regime, who tortured and hanged the finest representatives of the Hungarian people, tried to re-establish the authority of the capitalists and landowners of Hungary. In
55 Budapest and other Hungarian towns order is being restored, the resistance of negligible groups of insurgents in Budapest is being crushed with the active participation of the Hungarian popula-
60 tion. . . .

[*9:05* P.M.] This morning the forces of the reactionary conspiracy against the Hungarian people were crushed. A new Hungarian Revolutionary Worker-
65 Peasant Government, headed by the Prime Minister Janos Kadar, [yä'nôsh kä'dər], has been formed. The Government has appealed to the Hungarian people to ally its forces in defense of the
70 victories of the people's democratic system and for a final rout of the reac-

tionary conspirators. . . . The counter-revolutionary bands nesting in public buildings are being successfully
75 smashed and are capitulating. . . .

During 4 November events have led to a complete defeat of the forces of counter-revolution. . . . The proclamation of the new Revolutionary Govern-
80 ment in Hungary has found a lively response among genuine patriots.

## Discussing the Reading

1. What kind of help did the Hungarians ask of the United Nations? What warning did the Hungarians give to the West?

2. Is the United States morally obligated to aid individuals. parties. or factions who seek freedom for their countries? Why or why not? Should U.S. foreign policy be based instead on pragmatic considerations? What would the United States have gained or lost by not aiding the Hungarians?

**CRITICAL THINKING**
**Evaluating Sources of Information**

Review Radio Moscow's response to the Hungarians' appeals for help. Cite specific words and phrases that portray the Soviets as rescuers of the civilian population against an "evil" armed rebellion.

# The Long March to Derry

**TIME FRAME**
*Late 1960s*

**GEOGRAPHIC SETTING**
*Northern Ireland*

In the late 1960s conflict developed in Northern Ireland between the Protestant majority and the Catholic minority. The Catholics claimed that they were often discriminated against in such areas as voting rights, jobs, and housing. Borrowing tactics from the American civil-rights movement, the Catholics first staged a series of nonviolent protest marches, including the 73-mile "long march" from Northern Ireland's capital, Belfast, to the city of Londonderry (or Derry) in January, 1969. Unfortunately, these early attempts at peaceful protests were soon succeeded by sectarian violence by both Catholics and Protestants that has continued up to the present and has resulted in thousands of deaths. The following account of the "long march" comes from *The Price of My Soul*, a memoir by Bernadette Devlin (1947–    ), one of the leaders of the civil-rights movement. Lines 1–55 describe an attack on the marchers by the "Paisleyites," the extremist Protestant faction led by the Rev. Ian Paisley. Lines 56–132 picture the arrival of the marchers in Derry. The "Internationale" [an ter nä syō näl'] referred to is a revolutionary song composed in France at the time of the Paris Commune in 1871.

A nd then we came to Burntollet Bridge, and from lanes at each side of the road a curtain of bricks and boulders and bottles brought the march
5 to a halt. From the lanes burst hordes of screaming people wielding planks of wood, bottles, laths, iron bars, crowbars, cudgels studded with nails, and they waded into the march. . . .
10  I was a very clever girl: cowardice makes you clever. Before this onslaught, our heads-down, arms-linked tactics were no use whatever, and people began to panic and run.
15 Immediately my mind went back to

Derry on October 5 [an earlier march] and I remembered the uselessness of running. As I stood there I could see a great big lump of flatwood, like a plank
20 out of an orange-box, getting nearer and nearer my face, and there were two great nails sticking out of it. By a quick reflex action, my hand reached my face before the wood did, and immediately
25 two nails went into the back of my hand. Just after that I was struck on the back of the knees with this bit of wood which had failed to get me in the face, and fell to the ground. And then my
30 brain began to tick. "Now, Bernadette," I said, "what is the best thing to do? If you leave your arms and legs out, they'll be broken. You can have your skull cracked, or your face destroyed." So I
35 rolled up in a ball on the road, tucked my knees in, tucked my elbows in, and covered my face with one hand and the crown of my head with the other. Through my fingers, I could see legs
40 standing round me: about six people were busily involved in trying to beat me into the ground, and I could feel dull thuds landing on my back and head. Finally these men muttered something
45 incoherent about leaving that one, and tore off across the fields after somebody else.

When everything was quiet, and five seconds had gone by without my feeling
50 anything, I decided it was time to take my head up. I had a wee peer round,

Looking weary but satisfied, Bernadette Devlin is shown after her 1969 election victory in the photograph on the facing page. In the photograph below, Devlin is shown with a group of Ulster children.

ducked again as a passing Paisleyite threw a swipe at me, and then got up. What had been a march was a shambles. . . .

As we approached Derry, we were met by the Radical Students' Alliance who had come out to meet us. They stood to attention, singing the "Internationale" with us, as we went past, then fell in to form the end of the march. They were the only people who did this: other supporters joining us forced their way into our ranks, but the Radical Students paid this homage to those of us who had come all the way from Belfast. The police had promised us more trouble before we reached the city center, and as we drew level with the first houses, Eamonn McCann [another civil-rights leader] got up on a chair to call through a megaphone: "Remember we have marched seventy-three miles. Please don't let violence mar the end of the march. If you're attacked, just keep marching.'' The march went by, Eamonn was left there all on his own, and a wee Paisleyite ran out and thumped him; so Eamonn, of course, took to his heels and ran and found the rest of the march again. We came abreast of Altnagelvin Hospital, and all our people who could hobble out, hobbled into the front rows with their bandages, and so, two thousand strong, we rounded the corner and came down the hill to the walled city of Derry.

A bonfire was waiting for us in Irish Street, to burn such of our banners as had survived Burntollet Bridge. Again the march was met by a rain of stones, bricks, bottles, burning sticks from the bonfire, and petrol bombs. Fortunately the Paisleyites were very bad at making petrol bombs—most of the ones they threw simply didn't materialize. I could feel stones bouncing off my head, leaving me apparently undamaged, and I saw four hit Michael Farrell before he fell: he carries his blood-stained coat around with him to this day for the prestige of it. Farther down the road a squad of Paisleyites had got into a quarry behind the houses and were lobbing stones over the roofs. The police advised us to wait until the enemy ran out of ammunition, and this looked like being a long wait, for they had ammunition there for the next ten years. The marchers stood in against the houses to avoid the stones, which were coming flying over into the middle of the street, and overshooting to break windows in the houses opposite. Every time there was a lull, a few more marchers sprinted to safety, and bit by bit we all got past.

That was the last danger: now we were in Derry, and the people lined the streets and cheered. They'd put up a platform in Guildhall Square, and they wanted all of us on it at once: every time a few more were dragged up one side, several fell off at the other side. But the people wanted to hear something from all of us. That was when I called Derry "the capital city of injustice"—grand phrase: it flashed all over Ireland. It was impossible to describe the atmosphere, but it must have been like that on V-Day [the end of World War II]: the war was over and we had won; we hadn't lifted a finger, but we'd won.

## Discussing the Reading

1. Did Bernadette Devlin present herself as heroic in her account of the attack at the bridge? Explain.

2. What was important to Devlin about the marchers' success in reaching Derry?

### CRITICAL THINKING
### Assessing Cause and Effect

To what extent does protest depend upon the news media for success? Refer to the reading in your answer.

During China's brief outburst of free speech late in 1978, crowds in Beijing avidly read wall posters.

# China's "Democracy Wall"

**TIME FRAME**
*Late 1970s*

**GEOGRAPHIC SETTING**
*China*

In November, 1978, posters critical of Mao Tse-tung [mä′ō dzu′dùng′], chairman of the Chinese Communist Party from 1945 to 1976, began appearing on walls near Tiananmen [tē en′än mùn] Square, the main square of Beijing [bä′jing′], China. These first posters had the official approval of China's new leader Deng Xiaoping [dung′ shyou′ping′], and many were designed to discredit his opponents. In a rare outburst of free speech, however, posters began appearing daily in late November and early December which said critical things about China in general, and these clearly did not have official approval. Some were written on notebook paper; one was signed by a garage mechanic; one was by a student who complained about too much homework; others were by relatives of missing political prisoners. Most, however, were direct political criticism, as the following examples show. People gathered at what the American press dubbed "Democracy Wall" to read the political commentaries which the Chinese had not been allowed to express for decades. By late December, however, Deng Xiaoping felt free speech had gone far enough and the posters were torn down. While Deng did preside for the next ten years over China's general economic liberalization, he was also the one who ordered the military's bloody attack in June, 1989, on hundreds of thousands of demonstrators again demanding democracy in Tiananmen Square.

Chairman Mao, because his thinking was metaphysical thinking during his old age and for all kinds of other reasons, supported the "Gang of
5 Four" [short-lived ruling clique following Mao's death] in raising their hands to strike down Deng Xiaoping. [This was the first official poster. Those that followed were unofficial.]

He [Wang Dongxing, head of the Secret Police] blindly interfered and brought disaster to the masses. When the situation changed, he changed with the wind. . . . Blast him out, this insect.

Chairman Mao was a man, not a god. The time has come to give him his real place.

America is a capitalist country and is the most developed in the world. The United States is only 200 years old, but it has developed because [unlike China] it has no idols or superstitions.

There should be a social life other than meetings!

Comrades, the proletariat has to safeguard itself against its own deputies and officials, or in other words, people have to safeguard themselves against their leaders. Do you feel surprised when you hear this?

The great democratic and human rights to which we aspire have today raised their heads in the great land of China.

When one finally turns thirty and can get married, it should be possible to have a small room with a bed.

It would be un-Marxist to expect a revolutionary leader to be free of any short-comings. . . . Chairman Mao was our leader, but after all, did he not have his faults? Did his instructions not contain mistakes?

Human rights in China have suffered the most terrible attacks and are still totally denied. . . . The ghost of human rights will haunt China forever. . . . Throughout China, there are cases of wrongful persecution, injustice, hun-

ger, and forced separation of families. . . . We hope that you and President Carter will be even more concerned with the human rights movement in our country in the future. . . .

What kind of modernization does China plan to achieve? The Soviet, American, Japanese, or Yugoslav type? We the ordinary masses know nothing of these issues. . . . I work hard, even exceeding my quotas, but after my shift I just like to ponder what I have been working for. . . .

Deng should come here and read these wall-posters instead of apologizing for Chairman Mao's mistakes.

## Discussing the Reading

1. Consider that these posters are expressions of the writers' opinions. Is it accurate to say that the United States is without "idols or superstitions" (lines 19–22)? Do you believe that "people have to safeguard themselves against their leaders" (lines 27–29)? Do your opinions agree or disagree with those on "Democracy Wall"?

2. Read lines 44–54. What are human rights? Should an American president be concerned with human rights in China? Is your answer the same as the one you gave in relation to aid for Hungary (see Reading 35A, question 2)?

3. Why do you think Deng Xiaoping felt the need to stop the free speech at "Democracy Wall"?

### CRITICAL THINKING
### Making Generalizations

Many of the posters are criticisms of Chairman Mao. What other areas of life in China come under attack in these posters?

Inspired by America's Statue of Liberty, the "Freedom Goddess" was erected by Chinese students in Beijing's Tiananmen Square during their pro-democracy demonstrations early in 1989. Tens of thousands of people saw the statue before it was demolished by troops brought in to disperse the students.

# The First Servant of the Indian People

**TIME FRAME**
*Late 1940s*

**GEOGRAPHIC SETTING**
*India*

On August 15, 1947, India received its independence after centuries of British colonial rule. Its new leader was Jawaharlal Nehru [jə wä′hər läl′ nä′rü] (1889–1964), who had struggled for years to help India win its independence in a peaceful and democratic way. In his speech to the Indian people on that first independence day, excerpted below, he reminded them that in this moment when "the soul of a nation, long suppressed, finds utterance," not only joy and freedom, but work and commitment would be required of all.

F ellow countrymen, it has been my privilege to serve India and the cause of India's freedom for many years. Today I address you for the first
5 time officially as the First Servant of the Indian people, pledged to their service and their betterment. I am here because you willed it so and I remain here so long as you choose to honor me with
10 your confidence.

We are a free and sovereign people today, and we have rid ourselves of the burden of the past. We look at the world with clear and friendly eyes, and at the
15 future with faith and confidence.

The burden of foreign domination is done away with, but freedom brings its own responsibilities and burdens, and they can only be shouldered in the spirit
20 of a free people, self-disciplined, and determined to preserve and enlarge that freedom.

We have achieved much; we have to achieve much more. . . . The eyes of the
25 world are upon us watching this birth of freedom in the East and wondering what it means.

Jailed by the British several times for his nationalist activities, Jawaharlal Nehru, shown below, served as India's prime minister from 1947 until his death in 1964. On the right, some of India's poor receive alms.

Our first and immediate objective must be to put an end to all internal 30 strife and violence, which disfigure and degrade us and injure the cause of freedom. They come in the way of consideration of the great economic problems of the masses of the people which 35 so urgently demand attention.

. . . Today our people lack food and clothing and other necessaries, and we are caught in a spiral of inflation and rising prices. We cannot solve these 40 problems suddenly, but we cannot also delay their solution. So we must plan wisely so that the burdens on the masses may grow less and their standards of living go up. We wish ill to 45 none, but it must be clearly understood that the interests of our long-suffering masses must come first and every entrenched interest that comes in their way must yield to them. We have to 50 change rapidly our antiquated land-tenure system, and we have also to promote industrialization on a large and balanced scale, so as to add to the wealth of the country, and thus to the 55 national dividend which can be equitably distributed.

Production today is the first priority, and every attempt to hamper or lessen production is injuring the nation, and 60 more especially harmful to our laboring masses. But production by itself is not enough, for this may lead to an even greater concentration of wealth in a few hands, which comes in the way of prog-65 ress and which, in the context of today, produces instability and conflict. Therefore, fair and equitable distribution is essential for any solution of the problem.

70

## Discussing the Reading

1. Lines 28–35 allude to the sectarian violence that has plagued India since World War II. How can society permit religious freedom and yet still eliminate violent attacks by one religious group upon another?

2. On what areas did Nehru want the Indians to focus their attention?

3. Nehru said that freedom "brings its own responsibilities and burdens" and that self-discipline is necessary to handle freedom. What might some of these responsibilities be for a nation? For an individual?

### CRITICAL THINKING
### Recognizing Values

Nehru's speech was the expression of what he hoped to bring to India as its leader. What principles did he value most, as revealed in his speech?

# Kwame Nkrumah's Views on Independence

37A

**TIME FRAME**
*Late 1950s*

**GEOGRAPHIC SETTING**
*Ghana*

In 1957 the former British colony of the Gold Coast became the first sub-Saharan African colony to become independent. It took the name of Ghana [gä'nə], after the African empire of 400–1235 A.D. It had been led through a relatively peaceful transition to independence by its first prime minister, Kwame Nkrumah [kwä'mä en krü'mə](1909–1972). In those early years of optimism and hope, Kwame Nkrumah, in his *Autobiography,* spoke for millions of Africans who longed for the right to participate in their own political process. Only later did problems of

In a 1963 photograph, Kwame Nkrumah is shown listening intently to a speech. Overthrown by an army coup in 1966, Nkrumah fled to Guinea. He died in exile in 1972.

GHANA

development produce dictatorship and disappointment in Nkrumah's Ghana, as well as in many other African countries.

I n 1934 when I applied to the dean for admission to Lincoln University [Pennsylvania], I quoted from Tennyson's *In Memoriam:*

5    So many worlds, so much to do,
     So little done, such things to be.
This was to me then, as it still is today [1956], an inspiration and a spur. It fired within me a determination to equip
10 myself for the service of my country.

When I wrote that letter, however, I little knew that it would take ten years in America and two-and-a-half years in England, living almost as an exile, to
15 prepare for the struggle that has so far engaged me and which, after nearly eight years, has almost been won.

Those years in America and England were years of sorrow and loneliness,
20 poverty and hard work. But I have never regretted them because the background that they provided has helped me to formulate my philosophy of life and politics. At the end of my student days in
25 America I was offered lectureships in several Negro universities, including

Lincoln. This was certainly tempting; it promised an end to my struggle for existence, a pleasurable life without
30 worry in an atmosphere that I had long felt to be a part of me. But I could not dismiss from my mind, in a matter of a few days, the flame of nationalism that had been fanned and kept alight for
35 over ten years.

Independence for the Gold Coast was my aim. It was a colony, and I have always regarded colonialism as the policy by which a foreign power binds
40 territories to herself by political ties, with the primary object of promoting her own economic advantage. No one need be surprised if this system has led to disturbances and political tension in
45 many territories. There are few people who would not rid themselves of such domination if they could . . . .

I saw that the whole solution to [our] problem lay in political freedom for our
50 people, for it is only when a people are politically free that other races can give them the respect that is due them. It is impossible to talk of equality of races in any other terms. No people without a
55 government of their own can expect to be treated on the same level as people of independent sovereign states. It is far better to be free to govern or misgovern yourself than to be governed by any-
60 body else . . . .

Once this freedom is gained, a greater task comes into view. All dependent territories are backward in education, in science, in agriculture, and in industry.
65 The economic independence that should follow and maintain political independence demands every effort from the people, a total mobilization of brain and manpower resources. What
70 other countries have taken three hundred years or more to achieve, a once dependent territory must try to accomplish in a generation if it is to survive.

## Discussing the Reading

1. Explain the meaning of the quotation from Tennyson's poem *In Memoriam.*

2. How did Kwame Nkrumah define colonialism? What conflicts does colonialism cause?

3. Review Reading 36B. How were the problems of India and Ghana similar? What qualities did Nehru and Nkrumah have in common?

**CRITICAL THINKING**
**Making Decisions**

Reread lines 48–60. Do you agree with Nkrumah that it is "far better to be free to govern or misgovern yourself than to be governed by anybody else"? What criteria would you use to evaluate whether or not a government governed well? Which independent African countries meet your criteria? Does the United States meet your criteria?

# Remember Sharpeville

# 37B

**TIME FRAME**
*Late 1950s-early 1960s*

**GEOGRAPHIC SETTING**
*South Africa*

In the 1940s and 1950s, the white government of South Africa officially established apartheid [ə pärt′hāt], a policy of racial segregation used to maintain white control. One of the apartheid regulations required blacks and coloreds (people of mixed race) to constantly carry identity cards, or "passes." Failure to carry a pass could result in arrest. On March 21, 1960, an anti-apartheid group organized a peaceful protest. Throughout South Africa, blacks were to present themselves at police stations without their passes as a show of defiance to apartheid. Large crowds gathered outside police stations in many towns. Most of these crowds were peacefully dispersed, but in the town of Sharpeville in the northeastern part of the country, police opened fire on the demonstrators, killing 69 people and wounding 178. As one historian observes, "Sharpeville brought South Africa to a new stage in which the struggle between black and white was increasingly marked by terrorism on the one hand and brute force on the other." The following two poems are by the South African poet Dennis Brutus (1924–     ). Jailed for anti-apartheid activities in the early 1960s and banned from teaching or writing after his release, Brutus left South Africa in 1966 and has since lived in exile, largely in the United States.

## Sharpeville

What is important
about Sharpeville
is not that seventy died:
nor even that they were shot in the back
5 retreating, unarmed, defenceless

and certainly not
the heavy calibre slug
that tore through a mother's back
and ripped through the child in her
10  arms
killing it

Remember Sharpeville
bullet-in-the-back day
Because it epitomized oppression
15 and the nature of society
more clearly than anything else;
it was the classic event

Nowhere is racial dominance
more clearly defined
20 nowhere the will to oppress
more clearly demonstrated

what the world whispers
apartheid declares with snarling guns

151

the blood the rich lust after
25 South Africa spills in the dust

Remember Sharpeville
Remember bullet-in-the-back day

And remember the unquenchable will
for freedom
30 Remember the dead
and be glad

the warriors who secured the final
15 prize.

[John Nangoza Jebe: shot by the police
in a Good Friday procession in
Port Elizabeth 1956]

### Discussing the Reading

1. In his poem "Sharpeville," Dennis Brutus refers to the shootings as "the classic event" (line 17). Why does he feel this episode is so significant?

2. In both "Sharpeville" and "For a Dead African" Brutus deals with victims of police violence. What is similar about his emotional response in both poems?

**CRITICAL THINKING**
**Identifying Assumptions**

In the last stanza of "For a Dead African," Brutus observes that when South Africa's blacks have finally secured their freedom, "these nameless unarmed ones will stand beside/the warriors who secured the final prize." What do these lines suggest about Brutus's assumptions concerning the roles of violence and nonviolence in the struggle against apartheid?

### For A Dead African

We have no heroes and no wars
only victims of a sickly state
succumbing to the variegated sores
that flower under lashing rains of hate.

5 We have no battles and no fights
for history to record with trite remark
only captives killed on eyeless nights
and accidental dyings in the dark.

Yet when the roll of those who died
10 to free our land is called, without
surprise
these nameless unarmed ones will
stand beside

Victims of the Sharpeville massacre are shown on the right. Below is the South African poet Dennis Brutus, who has used his writing, in works like "For a Dead African" and "Sharpeville," to attack apartheid.

# Palestinians and Jews— the Strategy of Exile

**TIME FRAME**
*Late 1980s*

**GEOGRAPHIC SETTING**
*Israel*

Since 1948 hundreds of thousands of the former Palestinian Arab inhabitants of what had become Israel have been living in refugee camps, primarily in the West Bank and the Gaza Strip. The Israeli army occupied these two areas during the 1967 Mideast war, and since that time the Arab populations of the Occupied Territories—both those living in the refugee camps and the inhabitants of the Arab towns and villages there—have been under Israeli rule. Late in 1987, discontent among Palestinian Arabs in the Occupied Territories developed into an open rebellion, known as the *intifada* [in-tə fä′dä; Arabic meaning "uprising"]. Men, women, and children joined in strikes and stonings of Israeli soldiers. Despite shootings, beatings, and arrests by the Israeli army, the demonstrations have continued up to the present. In 1987, before the outbreak of the intifada, a young Israeli writer named David Grossman (1954–   ) made a seven-week tour through the West Bank, which he recorded in his book *The Yellow Wind*. In the following excerpt from the opening chapter of *The Yellow Wind*, Grossman described his visit to the Deheisha [də-hī′shə] refugee camp.

O n a day of turbid rain, at the end of March, I turn off the main road leading from my house in Jerusalem to Hebron, and enter the Deheisha refugee
5 camp. Twelve thousand Palestinians live here in one of the highest population densities in the world; the houses are piled together, and the house of every extended family branches out in
10 ugly cement growths, rooms and niches, rusty iron beams spread throughout as sinews, jutting like disconnected fingers.

In Deheisha, drinking water comes
15 from wells. The only running water is the rainwater and sewage flowing down the paths between the houses. I soon give up picking my way between the puddles; there is something ridicu-
20 lous—almost unfair—about preserving such refinement here, in the face of a few drops of filth.

Beside each house—a yard. They are small, fenced in with corrugated alu-
25 minum, and very clean. A large *jara* filled with springwater and covered with cloth stands in each yard. But every person here will tell you without hesitation that the water from the spring
30 of his home village was sweeter. "In Ain Azrab"—she sighs (her name is Hadija, and she is very old)—"our water was so clear and healthy that a dying man once immersed himself, drank a few mouth-
35 fuls, and washed—and was healed on the spot." She cocks her head, drills me with an examining gaze, and mocks: "So, what do you think of that?"

I discover—with some bafflement, I
40 admit—that she reminds me of my grandmother and her stories about Poland, from which she was expelled. About the river, about the fruit there. Time has marked both their faces with
45 the same lines, of wisdom and irony, of great skepticism toward all people, both relatives and strangers . . . .

A strange life. Double and split. Everyone I spoke to in the camp is
50 trained—almost from birth—to live this double life: they sit here, very much here, because deprivation imposes sobriety with cruel force, but they are also there. That is—among us. In the vil-
55 lages, in the cities. I ask a five-year-old boy where he is from, and he immediately answers, "Jaffa," which is today part of Tel Aviv. "Have you ever seen

Flying the flag of their new homeland, a boatload of Jewish refugees from Europe arrives in Israel in the late 1940s.

Jaffa?" "No, but my grandfather saw it."
His father, apparently, was born here, but his grandfather came from Jaffa. "And is it beautiful, Jaffa?" "Yes. It has orchards and vineyards and the sea." . . .

This is how the others answer me also. The Palestinians, as is well known, are making use of the ancient Jewish strategy of exile and have removed themselves from history. They close their eyes against harsh reality, and stubbornly clamping down their eyelids, they fabricate their Promised Land. "Next year in Jerusalem," said the Jews in Latvia and in Cracow and in San'a, and the meaning was that they were not willing to compromise. Because they had no hope for any real change. He who has nothing to lose can demand everything; and until his Jerusalem becomes real, he will do nothing to bring it closer. And here also, again and again, that absolute demand: everything. Nablus and Hebron and Jaffa and Jerusalem. And in the meantime — nothing. In the meantime, abandoned physically and spiritually. In the meantime, a dream and a void . . . .

Everything happens elsewhere. Not now. In another place. In a splendid past or a longed-for future. The thing most present here is absence. Somehow one senses that people here have turned themselves voluntarily into doubles of the real people who once were, in another place. Into people who hold in their hands only one real asset: the ability to wait.

And I, as a Jew, can understand that well.

## Discussing the Reading

1. Why does the old Palestinian woman remind David Grossman of his Polish grandmother?

2. What does Grossman mean by the "strategy of exile" which he says is practiced by both Palestinians and Jews?

**CRITICAL THINKING**
**Making Hypotheses**

Why might the attitudes associated with the "strategy of exile" make it more difficult to settle the disputes between the Palestinians and the Jews?

# Bedouins Confront the 20th Century

**TIME FRAME**
*Early 1930s*

**GEOGRAPHIC SETTING**
*Saudi Arabia*

At the time of World War I, the Arabian Peninsula was a part of the Turkish Empire. The defeat of Turkey in 1918 left several tribal leaders contending for supremacy in Arabia. During the 1920s and '30s, Abdul Aziz ibn Saud [ib′ən sä üd′] (1880–1953) defeated his rivals and unified Arabia, eventually giving his new monarchy the name "Saudi Arabia." The political unification of Saudi Arabia coincided with the discovery of its enormous oil reserves. Vast wealth resulting from the sale of its oil poured into Saudi Arabia and drastically altered the traditional society of its Bedouin inhabitants. In the course of a few decades, Saudi Arabia's nomad population became 80 percent urban. The trilogy *Cities of Salt* by the contemporary Saudi novelist Abdelrahman Munif [äb′dəl rä män′ mü nēf′] (1933–      ) recounts the story of the emergence of cities in the Arabian Peninsula and the consequent destruction of the Bedouins' centuries-old way of life. The following excerpt from *Cities of Salt* comes from one of the early chapters of the trilogy and deals with the period of the discovery of oil in the early 1930s. The main character in this section of Munif's work is Miteb al-Hathal

[mi teb′ äl hä thäl′], inhabitant of a famous desert oasis, Wadi al-Uyoun [wad′ē äl ü yün′]. He is watching the strange actions of three Americans, who claim to be searching for water, but later turn out to be petroleum engineers.

---

T hey were busy all day long. They went places no one dreamed of going. They collected unthinkable things. They had a piece of iron—no one knew what it was or what they did with it—and when they returned in the evening they brought with them bags of sand and pieces of rock. Once they brought tamarisk and wormwood branches, and bunches of clover. They broke the branches in a strange way and attached pieces of paper on which they had written obscure things. That was not all: they placed wooden markers and iron poles everywhere they went, and wrote on them, and wrote things no one understood on the sheets of paper they carried with them every-

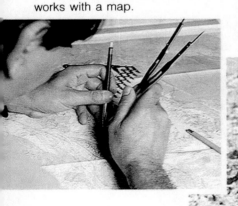

Methodical and tireless, geologist Max Steineke, shown on the right, was one of the first to explore Saudi Arabia for oil in the 1930s. Below, a modern Saudi oil engineer works with a map.

where. The markers were hidden or moved around whenever they went away—the boys of the wadi moved and gathered up some of the markers, and the grown-ups did nothing to stop them. When Fawaz [fä wäz′; Miteb's son] showed up with some of the iron poles after he had been tending the sheep, his father scrutinized them carefully and a little fearfully. He knocked them on a rock, knocked them against the other and listened to them for a long time, then he said that they must not be brought near the fire.

And the water. Where was the water and how could they find it? Did the government know where they were and what they were doing? When Miteb al-Hathal asked him, Ibn Rashed [ib′ən rä shed′] said that they had a certificate from the emir [ə mir′; the local ruler] and had been his guests for a week. When Miteb asked the two guides, they said that the emir had sent them and that was why they had come.

Miteb al-Hathal grew more pessimistic with every passing day; his fears mounted and his curses were more frequent. He came to talk about nothing else. If all the men joined him in discussing the problem, not all of them agreed with him, but because of his age and social standing they let him think and swear as he pleased.

He sensed that something terrible was about to happen. He did not know what it was or when it would happen, and he took no comfort in the explanations offered him from all sides. The very sight of the foreigners and their constant activity all day, the instruments they carried around, the bags of sand and stones they had amassed after writing in their notebooks and drawing symbols on them, the discussions that lasted from sundown until after supper and the writing that followed, the damned questions they asked about dialects, about tribes and their disputes, about religion and sects, about the routes, the winds, and the rainy seasons—all these caused Miteb's fear to grow day by day that they meant to harm the wadi and the people. The wadi's inhabitants, who at first viewed the three foreigners with scorn and laughed when they saw them carrying bags of sand and rock, grew more surprised when they discovered that the three knew a lot about religion, the desert, the bedouin's life, and the tribes. The [Islamic] profession of faith [the foreigners] repeated whenever they asked, and their scriptural citations, moved many people of the wadi to wonder among themselves if these were jinn [jin; supernatural beings], because people like them who knew all those things and spoke Arabic yet never prayed were not Muslims and could not be normal humans.

## Discussing the Reading

1. How do Miteb al-Hathal and Ibn Rashed differ in their response to the three Americans? Which of these two individuals would probably have a more difficult time adjusting to the urbanization of Bedouin society?

2. What aspects of the Americans' behavior do the inhabitants of the wadi find impossible to reconcile? To what conclusion does this lead them?

### CRITICAL THINKING
### Making Inferences

This passage from *Cities of Salt* shows an encounter between members of a pre-industrial society and modern technology. What can you infer from Miteb's behavior with the Americans' iron poles? What guesses does he make about their purpose?

# The Program of the Cuban Revolution

**TIME FRAME**
*Early 1960s*

**GEOGRAPHIC SETTING**
*Cuba*

In 1959, a revolution led by Fidel Castro (1927–    ) overthrew a corrupt dictatorship in Cuba. Under the communist dictatorship established by Castro, educational and health standards rose appreciably, as did living conditions among the peasantry, who comprised the great majority of the population. The professional and middle classes, however, suffered losses in both living standards and personal liberties, and many thousands fled to the United States. Castro described the goals of the Cuban revolution in a speech before the United Nations in September, 1960. The following are some excerpts from his speech.

W hat did the revolution find after it succeeded in Cuba? . . . Three million people, out of a total population of a little over 6 million, had no electric
5 light and enjoyed none of the benefits and comforts of electricity. Three and a half million people, out of a total population of a little over 6 million, were living in hovels and huts unfit for
10 human habitation. In the towns rents accounted for as much as one-third of family incomes. Electricity rates and rents were among the highest in the world.

15 Thirty-seven and a half percent of our population were illiterate, unable to read or write. Seventy percent of the children in the rural areas were without teachers. Two percent of our population
20 were suffering from tuberculosis, that is to say, 100,000 people out of a total of a little over 6 million. Ninety-five percent of the children in rural areas were suffering from diseases caused by para-
25 sites. Infant mortality was consequently very high. The average life span was very short. In addition, 85 percent of small farmers were paying rent for their lands amounting to as much as 30 per-
30 cent of their gross incomes, while $1\frac{1}{2}$ percent of all the landowners controlled

Posed with white doves of peace, Cuban leader Fidel Castro is shown making a speech in Havana early in 1959.

46 percent of the total area of the country. . . .

The National General Assembly of 35 the Cuban people condemns large-scale landowning as a source of poverty for the peasant and a backward and inhuman system of agricultural production; it condemns starvation wages and 40 the iniquitous exploitation of human labor by illegitimate and privileged interests; it condemns illiteracy, the lack of teachers, schools, doctors, and hospitals; the lack of assistance to the 45 aged in the American countries; it condemns discrimination against the Negro and the Indian; it condemns the inequality and the exploitation of women; it condemns political and military oli-50 garchies which keep our people in poverty, impede their democratic development and the full exercise of their sovereignty; . . . it condemns the imperialist monopolies and enterprises which 55 continually plunder our wealth, exploit our workers and peasants, bleed our economies and keep them backward, and subordinate Latin American politics to their designs and interests. . . .

60 Consequently, the National General Assembly of the Cuban people proclaims before America, and proclaims here before the world, the right of the peasants to the land; the right of the 65 workers to the fruits of their labor; the right of children to education; the right of the sick to medical care and hospitalization; the right of young people to work; the right of students to free voca-70 tional training and scientific education; the right of Negroes and Indians to full human dignity; the right of women to civil, social, and political equality; the right of the elderly to security in their 75 old age; the right of intellectuals, artists, and scientists to fight through their works for a better world; the right of States to nationalize imperialist monopolies, thus rescuing the national 80 wealth and resources.

## Discussing the Reading

1. Why would Castro's program have appealed to many Cubans?

2. Look at lines 60–80, which detail the rights of Cuban citizens. Which of these rights do U.S. citizens have? Which rights don't we have?

### CRITICAL THINKING
### Making Generalizations

The National General Assembly condemned conditions in Cuba. What generalizations can you make about the problems that faced the Cuban people? Based on your reading of the text (pages 745–746 in *History and Life*; pages 763–765 in *Living World History*), did the Cuban revolution solve them all?

# *Nunca Más* — Never Again

39B

**TIME FRAME**
*Late 1970s-early 1980s*

**GEOGRAPHIC SETTING**
*Argentina*

In 1976 the government of Argentina was suffering from an economic crisis and violence by political radicals. The military seized power and began a program of repression against any political opposition. Between 1976 and 1982 thousands of people were kidnapped by the military. Most were tortured, killed, and buried in secret graves. The mothers and sisters of these *desaparecidos* [de sä pä re sē′dōs; Spanish meaning "disappeared ones"] began to demonstrate silently every Thursday in the capital main square, the Plaza de Mayo.

Eventually the world press noticed these brave women and knowledge of the kidnappings spread. When the military government was finally overthrown in 1982, a commission was set up to investigate the disappearances. Many victims have still to be accounted for. The following selection is from the prologue to the commission's 500-page report called *Nunca Más* [nün′kä mäs; Spanish meaning "never again"].

D uring the 1970s, Argentina was torn by terror from both the extreme right and the far left. This phenomenon was not unique to our
5 country. Italy, for example, has suffered for many years from the heartless attacks of Fascist groups, the Red Brigades, and other similar organizations. Never at any time, however, did that
10 country abandon the principles of law in its fight against these terrorists, and it managed to resolve the problem through the normal courts of law, guaranteeing the accused all their rights of a
15 fair hearing.

"Mothers of the Plaza de Mayo" in Buenos Aires in June, 1982, on the eve of a visit to Argentina by Pope John Paul II. The photographs they wear suspended from their necks are those of missing relatives.

The same cannot be said of our country. The armed forces responded to the terrorists' crimes with a terrorism far worse than the one they were com-
20 bating, and after 24 March, 1976 [when the military took over Argentina's government] they could count on the power and impunity of an absolute state, which they misused to abduct,
25 torture, and kill thousands of human beings. . . .

The abductions were precisely organized operations, sometimes occurring at the victim's place of work, sometimes
30 in the street in broad daylight. They involved the open deployment of military personnel, who were given a free hand by the local police stations. When a victim was sought out in his or her
35 home at night, armed units would surround the block and force their way in, terrorizing parents and children, who were often gagged and forced to watch. They would seize the persons they had
40 come for, beat them mercilessly, hood them, then drag them off to their cars or trucks, while the rest of the unit almost invariably ransacked the house or looted everything that could be carried.
45 The victims were then taken to a chamber over whose doorway might well have been inscribed the words Dante read on the gates of Hell: "Abandon hope, all ye who enter here."
50 Thus, in the name of national security, thousands upon thousands of human beings, usually young adults or even adolescents, fell into the sinister, ghostly category of the *desaparecidos*, a
55 word (sad privilege for Argentina) frequently left in Spanish by the world's press. . . .

All sectors fell into the net: trade union leaders fighting for better wages;
60 youngsters in student unions; journalists who did not support the regime; psychologists and sociologists simply

for belonging to suspicious professions; young pacifists, nuns, and priests who had taken the teachings of Christ to shanty areas; the friends of these people, too, and the friends of friends, plus others whose names were given out of motives of personal vengeance, or by the kidnapped under torture. . . .

We have discovered close to 9,000 of these unfortunate people who were abandoned by the world. We have reason to believe that the true figure is much higher. Many families were reluctant to report a disappearance for fear of reprisals. Some still hesitate, fearing a resurgence of these evil forces. . . .

In the course of our investigations we have been insulted and threatened by the very people who committed these crimes. Far from expressing any repentance, they continue to repeat the old excuses that they were engaged in a *dirty war,* or that they were saving the country and its Western, Christian values, when in reality they were responsible for dragging these values inside the bloody walls of the dungeons of repression. . . .

Great catastrophes are always instructive. The tragedy which began with the military dictatorship in March 1976, the most terrible our nation has ever suffered, will undoubtedly serve to help us understand that it is only democracy which can save a people from horror on this scale, only democracy which can keep and safeguard the sacred, essential rights of man. Only with democracy will we be certain that NEVER AGAIN will events such as these, which have made Argentina so sadly infamous throughout the world, be repeated in our nation.

## Discussing the Reading

1. What conditions in the 1970s provided the opportunity for this campaign of terror? What could have stopped this campaign at that time?

2. What comparisons can you make between Nazi Germany in the 1930s and Argentina in the 1970s?

**CRITICAL THINKING**
**Making Inferences**
Lines 92–100 speak of the "essential rights of man." What are these essential rights?

# A World Economy

# 40A

**TIME FRAME**
*Late 20th century*

**GEOGRAPHIC SETTING**
*The world*

The 20th-century trend toward a global society, one in which countries have become more and more dependent upon each other economically, politically, and environmentally, intensified in the 1980s. The areas of business and trade touched the lives of people in both developed and developing countries as the highly industrialized nations searched for new markets and sources of raw materials and the developing nations attempted to develop technologies to feed their growing populations and to industrialize their economies.

The political cartoons on page 161 point out some key issues in this new world economy. The first deals with the widening gap between rich and poor countries. Even though the developing nations account for about half of the world's population, they produce and consume very little of the world's goods and services. Attempts to industrialize their economies often have not dealt with

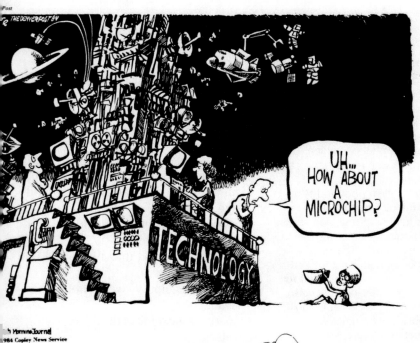

UH.... HOW ABOUT A MICROCHIP?

TECHNOLOGY

their primary concern—the survival of their people. The second cartoon illustrates the recent trend in Communist countries to introduce some free enterprise into their state-controlled economies in order to compete with the more successful Western nations. The third cartoon deals with the relationship between the United States and Japan in trade, satirizing what the cartoonist feels is the one-sided nature of Japan's trade policy.

## Discussing the Reading

1. Who or what is the "target" of the first cartoon? Why have they been selected as a target?

2. What are some of the possible results of China's experiments with capitalism?

### CRITICAL THINKING
### Analyzing Information

In the cartoon about U.S.-Japanese trade relations, which country is having difficulty with the relationship? How do you know? What is the cause of this difficulty, according to the cartoonist?

"We have a new landmark since we started our experiments with capitalism...
It's the Great Mall of China..."

DRAPER HILL
Courtesy Detroit News

# A Vision of the Future

**TIME FRAME**
*Imaginary Future*

**GEOGRAPHIC SETTING**
*Earth*

Futurists are thinkers who use scientific methods to theorize about what the world will be like in the years to come. Operating from differing assumptions, futurists create very different visions of the world of tomorrow, ranging from technological utopias to nightmare visions of the earth ravished by environmental pollution or nuclear war. The Scottish poet and literary critic Edwin Muir [myür] (1887–1959) was not a futurist in any technical sense, but the imaginary tomorrow that he describes in his poem "The Horses" displays a number of significant futurist themes. Written in 1956, during a period of the Cold War, when tensions between the United States and the Soviet Union increased the possibility of nuclear war, Muir's poem is set in a future when a brief, but cataclysmic conflict has destroyed civilization. The humans that have survived have returned to a pre-industrial way of life.

## The Horses

Barely a twelvemonth after
The seven days war that put the
world to sleep,
Late in the evening the strange horses
5   came.
By then we had made our covenant with
silence,
But in the first few days it was so still
We listened to our breathing and were
10   afraid.
On the second day
The radios failed; we turned the knobs;
no answer.
On the third day a warship passed us,
15   heading north,
Dead bodies piled on the deck. On the
sixth day
A plane plunged over us into the sea.
Thereafter
20 Nothing. The radios dumb;

And still they stand in corners of our
kitchens,
And stand, perhaps, turned on, in a million rooms
25 All over the world. But now if they
should speak,
If on a sudden they should speak again,
If on the stroke of noon a voice should
speak,
30 We would not listen, we would not let it
bring
That old bad world that swallowed its
children quick
At one great gulp. We would not have it
35   again.
Sometimes we think of the nations lying
asleep,
Curled blindly in impenetrable sorrow,
And then the thought confounds us
40   with its strangeness.
The tractors lie about our fields; at evening
They look like dank sea-monsters
couched and waiting.
45 We leave them where they are and let
them rust:
'They'll moulder away and be like other
loam.'
We make our oxen drag our rusty
50   ploughs,
Long laid aside. We have gone back
Far past our fathers' land.

                  And then, that evening
Late in the summer the strange horses
55   came.
We heard a distant tapping on the road,
A deepening drumming; it stopped,
went on again
And at the corner changed to hollow
60   thunder.
We saw the heads
Like a wild wave charging and were
afraid.

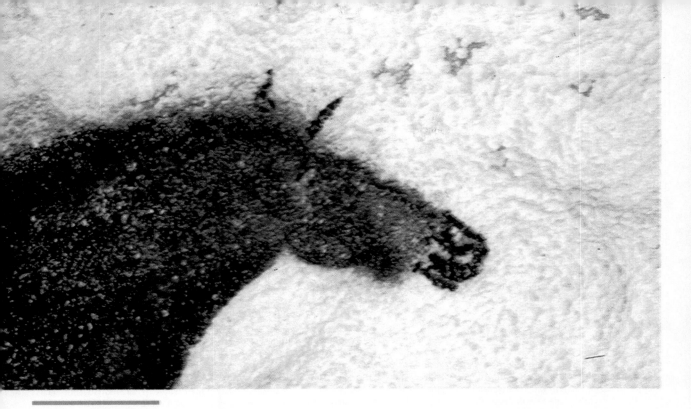

At once both familiar and strange, this twenty-thousand-year-old painting of a horse from the cave of Lascaux in southern France conveys the beauty and mystery of animals.

We had sold our horses in our fathers'
65   time
To buy new tractors. Now they were
  strange to us
As fabulous steeds set on an ancient
  shield
70 Or illustrations in a book of knights.
We did not dare go near them. Yet they
  waited,
Stubborn and shy, as if they had been
  sent
75 By an old command to find our whereabouts
And that long-lost archaic companion-
  ship.
In the first moment we had never a
80   thought
That they were creatures to be owned
  and used.
Among them were some half-a-dozen
  colts
85 Dropped in some wilderness of the
  broken world,
Yet new as if they had come from their
  own Eden.
Since then they have pulled our ploughs
90 and borne our loads,
But that free servitude still can pierce
  our hearts.
Our life is changed; their coming our
  beginning.

## Discussing the Reading

1. How would the person who is speaking in Muir's poem feel if there were a possibility of returning to a world like the one which has ended?

2. How do the people react when the horses return? Why does the speaker say that the presence of the horses "can pierce our hearts"?

**CRITICAL THINKING**
**Identifying Assumptions**

Using "The Horses" as evidence, identify the assumptions of Muir the "futurist." Is he optimistic or pessimistic? Could he be said to have an ecological world view?

# Acknowledgments

## Source Readings

**1A** Mary Leakey, *Disclosing the Past.* Garden City: Doubleday & Company, Inc., 1984, pp. 120-121, 123. **1B** From *The Mountain Bushman of Basutoland* by Marion Walsham How (Pretoria, South Africa: J. L. Van Schaik Ltd., 1970). Reprinted by permission of the publishers. **2A** Samuel Noah Kramer, *History Begins at Sumer.* Garden City: Doubleday & Company, Inc., 1959, pp. 8-9. **2B** From Lichtheim, Miriam, *Ancient Egyptian Literature. Three Volumes,* pages 125-126. Copyright © 1973-1980 by The Regents of the University of California. Reprinted by permission of The University of California Press. **3A** From The Holy Bible, 1 Samuel 8:1, 3-6, 11-22. **3B** Daniel David Luckenbill, *Ancient Records of Assyria and Babylonia,* Vol. II. New York: Greenwood Press, Publishers. **4A, 5B, 6A** Aubrey Stewart and George Long, trans., *Plutarch's Lives.* London: G. Bell & Sons, Ltd., 1914. **4B** Reprinted by permission of the publisher and The Loeb Classical Library from *Plutarch's Moralia,* Vol. IV, trans. Frank C. Babbitt, translator. Cambridge, Mass.: Harvard University Press, 1927. **5A** From *The Clouds* by Aristophanes, translated by William Arrowsmith. Copyright © 1962, 1980 by William Arrowsmith. Reprinted by arrangement with New American Library, a Division of Penguin Books USA Inc., New York, NY. **6B** From *Roman Civilization, Volume II The Empire* by Naphtali Lewis and Meyer Reinhold. Copyright 1955 by Columbia University Press, pages 227-228. **7A** From the *Bhagavad Gita* translated by Juan Mascaró (Penguin Classics, 1962). Copyright © 1962 by Juan Mascaró. Reprinted by permission of Penguin Books Ltd. **7B** From *The Edicts of Asoka,* edited and translated by N. A. Nikam and Richard McKeon. Copyright © 1959 by The University of Chicago. Reprinted by permission of The University of Chicago Press. **8A** From *Sources of Chinese Tradition,* Vol. I, edited by Wm. Theodore de Bary. Copyright © 1960 Columbia University Press. Used with permission. **8B** Extract taken from *The Life and Times of Po Chü-i* by Arthur Waley. Reproduced by kind permission of Unwin Hyman Ltd. **9A** Letter from Bouba from "Pitoa — Pilot School in a Cameroon Village" by Rene Caloz. Reprinted by permission from the *Unesco Courier,* September 1960. "In Praise of Ironsmith" from *Shona Praise Poetry* compiled by Aaron C. Hodza, edited and translated by George Fortune Copyright © 1979 by Oxford University Press. Reprinted by permission of Oxford University Press, Oxford, England. **9B** From *Popul Vuh: The Definitive Edition of the Mayan Book of the Dawn of Life and the Glories of Gods and Kings,* translated by Dennis Tedlock. Copyright © 1985 by Dennis Tedlock. Reprinted by permission of Simon & Schuster, Inc. **10A** Excerpted by permission of the publishers and The Loeb Classical Library from *Eusebius: The Ecclesiastical History,* Vol. I, trans. Kirsopp Lake, Cambridge, Mass.: Harvard University Press, 1926. **10B** From "The Life of Charlemagne" by Einhard, from *Two Lives of Charlemagne* by Einhard and Notker the Stammerer, translated by Lewis Thorpe (Penguin Classics, 1966), copyright © Lewis Thorpe, 1966, pp. 74-9. Reproduced by permission of Penguin Books, Ltd. **11A** From *Gesta Francorum (The Deeds of the Franks)* Edited by Rosalind Hill. Copyright © 1962 by Rosalind Hill. Reprinted by permission of Oxford University Press. **11B** David Herlihy, *Medieval Culture and Society.* New York: Harper & Row, 1968, pp. 205-207. From *Life and Works of Saint Bernard, Abbot of Clairvaux, Second Edition,* Volume II, edited by Dom John Mabillon, translated and edited by Samuel J. Eales. Reprinted by permission of Burnes & Oates Limited. **12A** Elizabeth Kimball Kendall, ed., *Source Book of English History.* New York: Macmillan Publishing Company, 1900. **12B** Reprinted from *The Prince* by Niccolò Machiavelli, translated and edited by Robert M. Adams. A Norton Critical Edition. With the permission of W. W. Norton & Company, Inc. Copyright © 1977 by W. W. Norton & Company, Inc. **13A** *Procopius,* with an English translation by H. B. Dewing, Vol. I. New York: Macmillan Publishing Company, 1914. **13B** Adapted from *Medieval Russia's Epics, Chronicles, and Tales* edited and translated by Serge A. Zenkovsky. Copyright © 1963 by Serge A. Zenkovsky. Reprinted by permission of the publisher, E. P. Dutton, a division of Penguin Books USA Inc. **14A** N. J. Dawood, translator, *The Koran.* Baltimore: Penguin Books, 1968, pp. 216-218. **14B** From Gabrielli, Francesco, *Arab Historians of the Crusades — Selected and Translated from the Arabic Sources,* trans./ed. by Costello, E. J., pp. 120-123. Copyright © 1969 Routledge & Kegan Paul Ltd. Reprinted by permission of The University of California Press. **15A** From *Islamic Literature* by Najib Ullah, p. 38. Copyright © 1963 by Najib Ullah. Reprinted by permission of Washington Square Press, a division of Simon & Schuster, Inc. From "On Leaving Baghdad" in *Islamic Literature* by Najib Ullah. Copyright © 1963 by Najib Ullah. Reprinted by permission of Washington Square Press, a division of Simon & Schuster, Inc. **15B** From *Science and Civilization in Islam* by Sayyed Hossein Nasr. Copyright © 1968 by Sayyed Hossein Nasr. Reprinted by permission of the author. **16A** From *The Book of Ser Marco Polo: The Venetian Concerning the Kingdoms and Marvels of the East,* translated and edited by Colonel Sir Henry Yule, Vol. I (New York: Charles Scribner's Sons, 1929). Reprinted by permission of John Murray (Publishers) Ltd. **16B** From *The Heritage of Vietnamese Poetry,* edited and translated by Huynh Sanh Thong (Yale University Press, 1979). Reprinted by permission of Huynh Sanh Thong. **17A** "The Death of Atsumori" from *Anthology of Japanese Literature* by Donald Keene. Copyright © 1955 by Grove Press. Reprinted by permission of Grove Weidenfeld. **17B** Excerpts from *The Book of Tea* by Okakura Kakuzo. Copyright © 1956 by Charles E. Tuttle Co., Inc. Reprinted by permission of Charles E. Tuttle Co., Inc., Tokyo, Japan. **18A** From *Sundiata: An Epic of Old Mali* by D. T. Niane, translated by C. D. Pickett. Reprinted by permission of the publisher, Longman Group Limited. **18B** L. S. Stavrianos, ed., *The Epic of Modern Man.* Englewood Cliffs: Prentice-Hall, Inc., 1966, pp. 72-74. **19A** John Addington Symonds, Trans., *The Autobiography of Benvenuto Cellini.* New York: Random House, pp. 112-114. **19B** From *Lives of the Artists* by Giorgio Vasari, translated by George Bull (Penguin Classics, 1965). Copyright © 1965 by George Bull. Reprinted by permission of Penguin Books

Ltd. **20A** From *A Journal of the First Voyage of Vasco Da Gama, 1497-1499*, translated and edited by E. G. Ravenstein. Reprinted by permission of the Hakluyt Society. **20B** Excerpts from pp. 222-224 in *The Fugger News-Letters*, edited by Victor von Klarwill, authorized translation by Pauline de Chary. **21A** From "The Speech of Dr. Martin Luther before the Emperor Charles and Princes at Worms." Reprinted from *Luther's Works, Vol. 32*, Copyright © 1958 Muhlenberg Press, by permission of Augsburg Fortress. **21B** James Harvey Robinson, *Readings in European History*, Vol. II. Boston: Ginn and Company, 1906. **22A** From *Discoveries and Opinions of Galileo* by Galileo Galilei, translation by Stillman Drake, translation copyright © 1957 by Stillman Drake. Used by permission of Doubleday, a division of Bantam, Doubleday, Dell Publishing Group. **22B** William Harvey, *An Anatomical Disquisition on the Motion of the Heart and Blood in Animals*. Robert Willis, trans. London: J. M. Dent & Sons Ltd., 1907. **23A** From *The Turkish Letters of Ogier Ghiselin de Busbecq*, translated by Edward Seymour Forster (1927). Reprinted by permission of Oxford University Press. **23B** F. G. Talbot, *Memoirs of Babur Emperor of India: First of the Great Moguls*. London: Arthur L. Humphrey's, 1909. **24A** From *Emperor of China: Self-portrait of K'ang-hsi*, by Jonathan D. Spence. Copyright © 1974 by Jonathan D. Spence. Reprinted by permission of Alfred A. Knopf, Inc. and the author. **24B** Boxer, Charles. *Christian Century in Japan, 1549-1650*, from Appendix VII, "Text of the Sakoku, or Closed country edict of June, 1636." Copyright © 1951, 1979 Charles Boxer. Reprinted by permission of The University of California Press. **25A** Friar Diego de Landa, *Yucutan: Before and After the Conquest*, translated by William Gates, Dover Publications, Inc., New York, 1978. **25B** From *Introduction to Contemporary Civilization in the West*, Vol. I, Third Edition. Copyright © 1960 Columbia University Press. Used with permission. **26A** C. H. Firth, ed., *The Memoirs of Edmund Ludlow*, Oxford: Clarendon Press, 1894. **26B** From "A Bill for Establishing Religious Freedom" from the 1784 Report of the Committee of Revisors of Thomas Jefferson. **27A** From *The Press in the French Revolution* by J. Gilchrist and W. J. Murray. © Ginn & Company Ltd. Reprinted by permission **27B** Michael C. Meyer and William L. Sherman, *The Course of Mexican History*. New York:

Oxford University Press, 1979. **28A** J. F. C. Harrison, ed. *Society and Politics in England, 1780-1960*. New York: Harper & Row, 1965, pp. 70-72. **28B** *Gedenkbuch 20 Jahre Österreichische Arbeiterinnenbewegung*, ed. Adelheid Popp (Vienna, 1912), pp. 107-109. **29B** Gideon Lang, *The Aborigines of Australia in their Original Condition and their Relations with the White Man*, Melbourne, 1865, pp. 3-5, 37-41. **30A** Joseph Chamberlain, M. P., *Foreign & Colonial Speeches*. London: George Routledge & Sons, 1897. **30B** Excerpt from *Growing: An Autobiography of the Years 1904-1911* by Leonard Woolf. Copyright © 1961 by Leonard Woolf. Reprinted by permission of Harcourt Brace Jovanovich, Inc. **31A** From *The World of Yesterday*, An Autobiography by Stefan Zweig (New York: Viking Press, 1943). Reprinted by permission of Atrium Press Ltd. and Cassell PLC, London. **31B** The material from *Testament of Youth* by Vera Brittain is included with the permission of her literary executors. Published by Virago Press, Ltd. **32A** N. S. Trusova et al, eds., *Natchalo Pervoi Russkoi Revoliutsii, Yanvar'-Mart 1905 Goda*. AN SSSR, Moscow, 1955, No. 21, pp. 28-31. **32B** From *On Stalin and Stalinism* by Roy A. Medvedev, translated by Ellen de Kadt. Copyright © 1979 by Roy A. Medvedev. English translation copyright © 1979 by Oxford University Press. Reprinted by permission of Oxford University Press. **33B** from *Restless Days: A German Girl's Autobiography* by Lilo Linke. Copyright 1935 by Alfred A. Knopf, Inc. and renewed 1963 by Lilo Linke. Reprinted by permission of Alfred A. Knopf, Inc. and Cuero y Calcedo. **34A** Excerpts from the speech, "A total and unmitigated defeat," October 5, 1938, by Winston Churchill to the House of Commons, as recorded in *Hansard*, the Official Report of House of Commons Debates. **34B** From *Memoirs of Harry S. Truman, Volume One: Year of Decisions*. Copyright © 1955 by Time Inc. Reprinted by permission of Stinson, Mag, & Fizzell for the Estate of Harry S. Truman. **35A** Cited in Melvin J. Lasky, editor, *The Hungarian Revolution: The Story of the October Uprising as Recorded in Documents, Dispatches, Eye-Witness Accounts, and World-Wide Reactions*. New York: Frederick A. Praeger, 1957, pp. 238-240. **35B** From *The Price of My Soul* by Bernadette Devlin. Copyright © 1969 by Bernadette Devlin. Reprinted by permission of Alfred A. Knopf, Inc. and Andre Deutsch Ltd. **36A**

"China's War of Words," *Newsweek*, December 4, 1978, p. 83. "China's Winds of Change" by David Butler, *Newsweek*, December 11, 1978, p. 43. Kwan Ha Yim, ed., *China Since Mao*. New York: Facts on File, 1980, pp. 124-125. James D. Seymour, ed., *The Fifth Modernization: China's Human rights Movement, 1978-1979*. Standfordville, New York: Human Rights Publishing Group, 1980. p. 20. Andrew J. Nathan, *Chinese Democracy*. New York: Alfred A. Knopf, 1985, p. 13. David S. G. Goodman, *Beijing Street Voices: The Poetry and Politics of China's Democratic Movement*. Boston: Marion Boyars, 1981, p. 65. **36B** Excerpt from *Independence and After* by Jawaharlal Nehru. Copyright 1950 by John Day & Co. Reprinted by permission of Harper & Row, Publishers, Inc. **37A** From *The Autobiography of Kwame Nkrumah*. Copyright and all rights reserved Panaf Books, 57 Caledonian Road, London NI 9BU. **37B** "Sharpeville" from *Stubborn Hope* by Dennis Brutus. Copyright © 1978 by Dennis Brutus. Reprinted by permission of the author. "For a Dead African" from *A Simple Lust* by Dennis Brutus. Copyright © 1973 by Dennis Brutus. Reprinted by permission of Hill and Wang, a division of Farrar, Straus & Giroux, Inc. and William Heinemann International. **38A** Excerpt adapted from "A Man Is Like a Stalk of Wheat" from *The Yellow Wind* by David Grossman. Copyright © 1988 by David Grossman and Koteret Rashit. English translation copyright © 1988 by Haim Watzman. Reprinted by permission of Farrar, Straus & Giroux, Inc. **38B** From *Cities of Salt* by Abdelrahman Munif. Copyright © 1987 by Abdelrahman Munif. Reprinted by permission of Vintage Books, a Division of Random House, Inc. **39A** United Nations. *Official Records of the General Assembly*. Fifteenth Session. Part I, Vol. I (1960), pp. 117-136. **39B** Excerpts from *Nunca Más: The Report of the Argentine National Commission on the Disappeared*. Translation Copyright © 1986 by Writers and Scholars International Ltd. Reprinted by permission of Farrar, Straus and Giroux, Inc. **40B** "The Horses" from *Collected Poems* by Edwin Muir. Copyright © 1960 by Willa Muir. Reprinted by permission of Oxford University Press and Faber and Faber Ltd.

**Illustrations**

Illustration not credited is from Scott, Foresman. **Cover:** Pala d'Oro (detail)